THE BEGINNING FROM THE END

WHY GENESIS?

THE BEGINNING FROM THE END

WHY GENESIS?

DR. CORBETT GAULDEN

RAVEN'S food

Publisher—Raven's Food

Raven's Food
6717 Matador Ranch Road
North Richland Hills, TX 76182
Email: theravensfood@gmail.com

Library of Congress Cataloging-in-Publication Data
Library of Congress Control Number: 2017916831

ISBN: 979-8-9862133-5-4 Paperback
      979-8-9862133-0-9 eBook

DEDICATION

A number of persons were quite influential in the decision to write the present work. It was a difficult undertaking and without their ongoing support, it would not have been possible. In particular, I want to offer thanks to the following:

Paul and Barbara Strange

Jamie and Cathy Hurst

Jerry and June Chapman

Jane Merrick

I am aware there are several very controversial passages in the book. These folks are not to blame for that. I am.

INVITATION

I wish to invite readers to an ongoing discussion on the variety of controversial topics which were touched upon in this book. To that end, we have arranged a discussion forum and an area for the presentation of longer, related topics which might be of interest.

https://ravensfood.com/books/BeginningFromTheEnd/Resources

TABLE OF CONTENTS

INTRODUCTION

The Bible itself, appropriately enough, opens with the first acts of creation. While it mentions nothing that preceded the first acts of creation, the very fact of creation presents at least three highly significant implications. First, the Creator, by necessity, must have existed before the acts of creation began. This must be so because no creation could occur apart from a pre-existing Creator. Second, if such a Creator exists, He must exist within a particular unique context of His own. One of the basic assumptions of this work is that precisely such an entity exists and that He is the One we call GOD. Since GOD existed prior to the beginning of the acts of creation, the context of His existence was not, is not, and cannot be the phenomenon we call The Creation. Instead, GOD has always existed in a context I choose to call herein The Eternal, at least to distinguish it from The Creation. From this we can deduce that GOD existed before The Creation in a context called The Eternal that was not and is not The Creation. Finally, the acts of creation and that which they produced were purposeful.

In summary of our analysis so far, we can assert four basic declarations:

1. There exists an entity called **GOD** who is the Creator of **The Creation.**

2. **GOD** pre-existed **The Creation.**

3. **GOD** existed, therefore, in a context called **The Eternal.**

    a) **The Eternal** pre-existed **The Creation**

    b) **The Eternal** remains independent of
        The Creation in every way.

    c) The **un-created substance** of **The Eternal** is the
        source of the **created substance** of **The Creation.**

4. **GOD** was **purposeful** in His acts of creation.

A corollary to these declarations is that what we call The Creation depends on The Creator for its existence and its character. It depends on nothing else and depends absolutely on The Creator. At the same time, neither The Creator nor The Eternal is in any way dependent on The Creation. The Creation exists at the pleasure of GOD the Creator. Everything that exists in The Creation was created out of the un-created substance of The Eternal. At the same time The Eternal is not in any whit diminished by the fact that the substances of The Creation were created out of its substance; it remains intact.

In this book we will examine the implications of this setting. If GOD existed in the context of The Eternal, why would He set out to bring The Creation into being? Was The Eternal too small or too boring for Him? This is one of the topics we will consider. Of course, we cannot presume to know the mind of GOD regarding such fundamental considerations, but we may certainly ask the questions and seek understanding. GOD has, in fact, preserved for us considerable information regarding these things. His relationship with us appears to be more important to Him than it does to most of us. So we will explore the fact that He wants us to know, but that the knowing must take place in the special context of our relationship with Him. It is my belief that the Bible has been kept for us, against the odds I might say, as a device for finding clues that answer such questions. Because GOD is simply so much greater than we comprehend, He produced for us a lot of the information we need. The rest is revealed when we diligently seek Him and His truth.

It is my strong contention that the Bible is not simply a collection of many stories. Rather, it is the record of the unfolding of the truth about GOD and His intentions for The Creation. Herein we will examine the first building blocks of that truth. GOD is and always has been purposeful. There is no aspect of the unfolded truth that is not useful to us in understanding the GOD who created us because He loves us.

Before He created us there was nothing to be known that could matter directly to us. No concept of what we are has ever existed outside of Him. We are the product of His mind and will. I contend that we are even more fundamentally the product of His love. Love was the first and most basic motivation for His actions that led to The Creation. Furthermore, the core reason for The Creation was mankind. GOD desired a creature that would love Him as a free and open choice. That is what He set out to do and that is what He did. He created a creation as the context within which we may choose to love Him and to be His sons as fully as any created thing can be.

We are human beings and created entities. There are things about us that simply do not pertain to anything else that has been created. Everything else that exists was created for the purpose that GOD might call us to become His sons in a love relationship.

The beginning of the Bible, by necessity, is concerned with how He got things started. He did not start in the middle, but at the very beginning. He always knew where this thing was going, however. The purposeful Creator created with the end in mind. He did not create us to see whether or not He could. He created us for a deliberate and most profound purpose—to love Him as sons in an eternal relationship that begins in the humblest of circumstances.

I have written previously on the promises GOD made to Abraham when it became time for a "holy nation" to come forth. In this present volume our examination concerns the phenomena that led us to that point in divine history. We did not come from nowhere, nor are we going to nowhere. It is my hope that you will find this analysis of the earliest material of benefit in your increasingly mature walk with the One who loved you so much from The Eternal that He decided to make a creation and put you into it to be His representative—a kind of viceroy.

This book seeks to provide a coherent analysis of the actual textual material in the first eleven chapters of Genesis. It is deliberately text-centered and not oriented toward philosophy. In some cases, though, theological considerations are provided as glue for the components. It is not primarily theological but it must consider GOD as the source of its basic underlying energy, because He is its cause.

CHAPTER ZERO

PRE-CREATION

This study is an examination of the first eleven chapters of the Old Testament book of Genesis. We will give especially close attention to unpacking the meaning of the rather cryptic presentation of the earliest matters involving human beings. The narrative of this opening portion of Genesis focuses on the insertion of human beings (man) into the context called The Creation. I say "insertion" because I do not believe human beings are some sort of cosmic accident. We are here because of God's deliberate design and intent. Of particular interest to us is to understand how these early chapters reveal The Creator's fundamental purpose for the creature called man. Genesis chapters 1-11 link the first moment of creation to God's declaration of intent in Genesis 12:1-3 to bring forth a "great nation" of His own design. This "great nation" is subsequently called a "holy nation" in Exodus 19:6, and is defined further in Revelation 5:9-10 as blood-purchased "men from every tribe and tongue and people and nation...to be a kingdom and priests to our God; and they will reign upon the earth." These scriptural linkages underlie the analysis which forms the core of this study.

Most of us tend to read the narrative material of the Bible in a very superficial manner. We often focus on certain extractions from this material for morality lessons, but this typically lifts them out of their full context, which easily results in misunderstanding the overall message. To be clear, the lessons learned in such activities are not wrong

1

per se but usually are isolated and limited in their meaning. One of my purposes in this book is to step back and locate the greater context, not by abandoning the more isolated aspects of the narrative but endeavoring to locate and integrate them into the larger context.

However, the narrative of Genesis begins with the inescapable observation that its primary Actor must have existed prior to His created works, which we shall call The Creation. In essence, GOD existed before He began to create. Hence, He existed in a context that previously had not included anything that was created. Again, for the sake of clarity, The Creator is GOD. GOD is more than what is implied in the term Creator, but all that The Creator is can be found in the person of GOD.

Because GOD existed before the acts of creation began, it should be worth our while to at least consider how that gives context to The Creation. It seems unreasonable to propose that The Creation is a cosmic accident of some kind. That kind of thinking supposes GOD to be in a laboratory somewhere in which He performs some act just to see what will happen, or that The Creation is simply some cosmic material that somehow was "spilled" accidentally. Even more unreasonable is the proposition that The Creation is a cosmic phenomenon that came about without the involvement of any conscious being. Such assertions are a serious insult to GOD. It is my contention that GOD was purposeful in every aspect of either The Eternal or The Creation. In the absence of any evidence to the contrary, this must be so. More to the point, this assertion guides my analysis in this work in its every aspect.

1. **The Creation** is a **deliberate** and **purposeful** work of **The Creator.**

2. A **"holy nation"** is the **central purpose** of creation.

The first declaration avows that GOD created The Creation deliberately. It was neither random nor an accident; no spilled test-tube. The second statement declares that when GOD created The Creation, He had a specific purpose in mind. Not only was the event not an accident, its full context was found in a purpose. I propose that the purpose of The Creator can be found in a rather straightforward manner. In fact, the purpose of The Creation can be found in the divine narrative that concerns The Creation. For our purposes, that fundamental purpose is found in Revelation 5: 9-10 when read in the light of Genesis 12:1-3. The latter passage predicts something called a "holy nation" while the former describes the dynamics of the fully realized establishment of that holy nation.

Now, it turns out that GOD is an entity beyond our comprehension. That is to be expected in a relationship between a creation and the creator of that creation. Any creation, by its nature, must be of a lower order than its source. At the same time, however, GOD created us as sentient creatures with the capability of interacting with and relating to Him. In fact, He chose to reveal Himself to us as a vital component of His purpose to build of us that holy nation of His interest and intent.

GOD "Revealed"

To a great extent, GOD's revelation of Himself to us is found in His declaration to Abram in Genesis 12:1-3:

> *Now the LORD said to Abram, "Go forth from your country, And from your relatives And from your father's house, To the land which I will show you; And I will make you a great nation, And I will bless you, And make your name great; And so you shall be a blessing; And I will bless those who bless you, And the one who curses you I will curse. And in you all the families of the earth will be blessed."*

Other aspects of GOD's self-revelation are also found in scripture. For example, while we do not know the content of their conversations, it seems GOD walked about in the context of Eden with the man and the woman after He had created them. Certainly, He made

3

Himself known to them in those conversations. Genesis 3:8-9 may imply regular contact of this kind. Even earlier we find His commandment to them regarding the caretaking of the earth (Gen. 1:28-30). Other revelations of His relationship to His new human creatures can be found in Genesis 2:15-17 as well.

These various glimpses found in the early part of the book of Genesis are primarily *operational* in nature. We will come back to them later in the book. The key passage for us now is the prophecy in Genesis 12. While we cannot say that GOD explicitly revealed His central purpose at that point, He did instruct Abram in such a way as to begin the revelation of that purpose, which we see as fulfilled in Revelation 5:9-10.[1] The 42 generations from Abraham to JESUS (see Mt. 1:17) are the preparation of a foundation for which the Revelation passage is the summary. Hence, the operational revelations in the first few chapters of Genesis are concerned more with the disposition of the new creatures than with their collective destiny. At the same time, though, we must also consider this to be a very focused narrative.

Aside from the central purpose of GOD, scripture also reveals something about the person of GOD in the Gospel of John: *"And the Word became flesh, and dwelt among us, and we saw His glory, glory as of the only begotten from the Father..."* (Jn. 1:14) Just a bit later we read:, *"For God so loved the world, that He gave His only begotten Son* (Jn. 3:16). The term "only begotten" in these passages refers to something completely unique. This was not *a* begotten, but *only* begotten. There could be only one such entity. Of course, we know that the term refers to the man JESUS, who was the only human ever born of a woman whose conception did not involve a man. That conception was "caused" by GOD Himself (see Lk. 1:34-35). John 1 clearly speaks of the same entity as does John 3. If John 3:16 refers to JESUS, as it must from the context, then John 1:14 must also speak of JESUS[2] and calls Him "the Word." The "only begotten" is then also the "Word" of GOD.

The very first verse of John's Gospel makes this clear: *"In the beginning was the Word, and the Word was with God, and the Word was God"* (Jn. 1:1). The Word is the same entity as the "only begotten Son," as we just saw. Verse 1 unequivocally equates the Word with GOD. At once, the Word was GOD and the Word was the only begotten Son of GOD. If both are true, then GOD must exist in some corporate state, implied by the term "Godhead" that we sometimes use. In other words, the Godhead entity manifests as both GOD the Father and GOD the Son (as well as GOD the Holy Spirit). Scripture gives us this particular glimpse into the person of GOD for a reason. Why would a concept so difficult to understand be revealed unless it was extremely important?

Man "Conceived"

We know of the fallibility of Man from the history of Man. GOD did not intend for Man to exist in a fallen state. He did, however, create Man in such a way that a fallen state was the alternative to some other state. This is not the place to fully develop the idea, but it would not be possible for any human to *choose* to be a son of GOD unless that same human could choose to *not* be a son of GOD. GOD's desired state for humans, then, is that state in which humans choose consistently to be sons of GOD, but GOD will not compel any human to accept that state. If we are not compelled to accept the desired state called a "son" of GOD, then it must be that another state is possible. We will call that state the "not-son" of GOD state. By default, the "not-son" of GOD state is deficient or "fallen" because it is not the state of being GOD wishes for humans. This is the essence of the fallibility of man.

Possible States of Being for Humans
a. **Son of GOD (desired)**
b. **"Not-son" of GOD (deficient)**

This is not the place for a full discussion, but the state of being called son of GOD is oriented toward perfection by the will and design of God. The state of being called "not-son" of God cannot result in perfection. It is by definition a "fallen" state because it is part of the package after the fall of Man in the Eden narrative. We cannot argue that Adam was created to be a fallen being, only that he was created with that possibility. Adam was not fallen until he chose to be a "not-son," even if he thought the choice was but for a moment. Let's be clear, Adam was created with no fault in him. God did not create imperfection. At the same time, Adam was created with the capability of introducing fault into himself through his choices. We'll save that for another chapter.

God knew fully before He began the acts of creation that when He made the man with the power to choose the state-of-being we just called "not-son," at some point a man would choose that state. In fact, in His omniscience, He knew from eternity past that the first man would make that choice. If God knew that fact, it must be true that God the Father knew that fact. In turn, God the Son knew it as well. This was before the fact. Both God the Father and God the Son knew when they created the human named Adam that he would decide on the "not-son" state at a certain point in time. As stated above, and as I will develop more fully momentarily, the *design* of God intended a *son* of God. It was also the *will* of God that the human being should enter into the state we have called "son of God."

Thus we are presented with a paradox. In order for God not to violate the will of any man (which would be tyrannical), He had to create Man in such a way that a man could choose to not be a son of God. At the same time, it was the design and will of God that a man would choose to be a son of God. God knew the wrong choice would be made, so He needed a remedy. One possibility was that a human could somehow work out by self-effort a conversion from the state of "not-son" to the state of "son." The procedures and rules for such a thing, however, would be eternally subject to efforts to negotiate it. Even if such accommodations could be worked out, there was the ever-present likelihood that yet another "not-son" choice would be made. This would cause the self-conversion event to be required endlessly.[3] Another approach would be to just forget the whole thing. But God chose yet another way. He chose to make provision by way of a process called "redemption."

GOD the Father and GOD the Son chose this redemption process to ensure the bringing into being of sons of GOD in spite of the existence of the possibility of the "not-son" choice. The way to "fix" the "not-son" problem was to provide redemption by way of a man who would never make the "not-son" choice. GOD the Father and GOD the Son knew that no man would be capable of such a life, one in which the "not-son" choice would never be made. In order to provide the "fix" for this situation, their personal participation was necessary. Hence, the plan of redemption through the intermediation of GOD the Son, in the person of JESUS the CHRIST (Messiah), was in place *before* the acts of creation began.[4]

The Purpose

So far we have only implied some things about the intention or purpose of GOD in this whole matter. The acts of creation were an intervention into an ongoing, eternal state that we must assume could well have continued indefinitely.[5] The Eternal did not seem to require The Creation for its existence or its continuity (another time word). Had the Godhead not decided to begin the acts of creation, they would not have happened and we would not be having this discussion!

This begs the fundamental question: Why did GOD create The Creation? When a volitional act is undertaken it requires a departure from the ongoing state of things. Certainly, when something as momentous as the creation of a universe is to take place it requires significant motivation. To answer our question we need to look at that motivation.

The primary *motivation* for GOD's acts of creation is *love*.

>   **a) The love of GOD desired an *object* of that love in addition to the Son of GOD:**
>
>   **b) *New* sons of GOD were created as *objects* of that love.**

7

In John 17, JESUS prays a very priestly prayer in the presence of His apostolic disciples. While that prayer has many dimensions, I believe the key to the whole prayer is found in verses 22-26. Verse 23 states that GOD has loved the disciples present with the same quality of love that He has for the Son. In verse 24 JESUS makes a remarkable statement, "...for you loved Me *before* the foundation of the world" (emphasis added). There it is. From before the foundation of the world, which we are herein calling the acts of creation, the Father had loved the Son with a quality of love the Son was now vouchsafing for us.

Let's consider that condition. In the context that existed before the acts of creation (foundation of the world), the Father loved the Son. This being the case, JESUS was here referring to the love of a father for a son in its purest and most perfect form. Even a superficial reading of the Gospels will reveal that the Son reciprocated the Father's love *as a son should love a father* in the purest and most perfect form. Verse 24 presents a very straightforward desire on the part of the Son to include the disciples in that relationship. In so doing, He was petitioning His Father to extend His pure and perfect Father-love to these disciples just as the Father had done for Him.[6]

When we consider these matters in light of the song of Revelation 5:9-10, we gain a coherent picture of the very purpose of GOD in the decision to bring The Creation into being. The Godhead set out to create sons who could become recipients of the love of GOD. The primary nature of GOD is as a Father. While the Son exists with the Father in the Godhead, it is the nature of things that the love of a father is primary to that of a son. The Father loves originally and the Son reciprocates. The love of the Son is a perfect reflection of the love of the Father. But the love of the Son is not the origin of the relationship. The Father does not reflect the love of the Son. It is the other way around. So, in the Godhead, the Father's love has the property of primacy over the Son's love and the Son reflects that back in some sense.

It must have been the expectation of the Godhead that when the love of GOD was extended to man it would be the love of a Father that was extended. The proper and desired response of a human being (man) would be to return that love to GOD the Father as an accurate reflection, just as GOD the Son had been doing in The Eternal before there was a creation into which man could be placed. This is our crux. When GOD (the Godhead) set about the acts of creation, His desire was that something would come to be that could become the object of His love as GOD the Father, just as had been GOD the Son, and, further, that this newly created object of His love would respond as had GOD the Son. However, that response could not be compelled. It had to be given freely in loving response as had been the response of GOD the Son. As we saw above, this lack of compulsion gave rise to the necessity of the possibility of a contrary response on the part of the something to be created. The Godhead, in omniscience, knew full well that the created something would fail in light of the choice. Redemption would be required.

Redemption would be painful because nothing in The Creation could bear its weight. The weight of redemption would have to be borne by the Godhead. They knew that. GOD the Father and GOD the Son knew before they began the acts of creation that the desired sons would need to be redeemed from the instances of "not-son" choices. In the "not-son" state, they would not be sons, but something else. To get back to the state of son, in which they would be capable of reflecting the love of GOD the Father, the Godhead would need to provide the method. The mechanics of that method would work from within the Godhead by necessity because the desired sons would not be capable. At this point the Godhead might well have decided to just forget the whole thing and co-exist in that perfect harmony of love that was theirs from eternity.

That is not what happened. In their eternal councils, they decided that the cost should be borne because of the value they would receive in the transaction. The desired sons would fail of their sonship because they could. Then the Godhead would redeem them at its own cost. In a sense, the perfect Son would be substituted for the fallen son. The cost of that, however, would be death for the perfect Son so that the substitution would be adequate to effectuate the redemption.

Inside the Godhead, the love of the Son for the Father was adequate to bring this bargain into being. It must be so that the value of that love relationship the two of them had together superseded even the highest cost in The Eternal. The love of GOD the Father for the Son was so great that He was willing to pay the highest price possible to gain other sons. The paradox was that the highest price possible was the life of that very Son. No higher bid could be made for a soul. No lesser bid would be adequate. GOD the Son also realized this was the most potent and powerful bargain that could be made. Out of His love for the Father, the Son undertook that payment as the proper reflection of His Father's love.

The Father and Son, co-existing in a perfect harmony of love, desired, out of the quality of that love, to extend it from its origin in the Father to an entire "nation" of sons. Those sons would need to be redeemed at the highest possible price so that nothing could prevent that redemption. Apparently, the desire of the two of them for this nation of sons was such a powerful force that it "caused" the acts of creation to be undertaken at the cost of the life of the Son in a flesh manifestation. And so, **suddenly**, the acts of creation began. The power of their reciprocal love caused them to convert uncreated substance into created substance. Suddenly, in a moment, it began. A kind of "bang" and the uncreated produced the created.[7]

The purpose of this book is to take a look at how this began to unfold once the Godhead acted to bring The Creation into being. We can better undertake that task now that we understand the motivation for the creative acts. There is a purpose for those creative acts, and that purpose is to bring forth "a kingdom and priests to our God" (Rev. 5:10). This kingdom, this nation, this holy nation, is the manifestation of the desired sons of GOD.

Let's turn our attention now to some of the details that attend the bringing forth of this phenomenon.

---

[1] C. Gaulden, *Birth of The Holy Nation, volume 1*, (Chambersburg, PA: eGenCo, 2015), explains this phenomenon fairly extensively.

² The man of flesh whose name was Jesus can be thought of as the vessel into which the Son of God (God the Son) came in order that the Son of God might be a flesh being for purposes of the Godhead. Any attempt on our part to fully understand the ramifications of this truth is destined to end in frustration. To simply say, as I do, that He was at once both fully human and the Son of God does not actually explain to the human mind how such a thing can be. Particularly, in light of the argument that "Son of God" or "God the Son" refers to an entity who existed prior to the commencement of the acts of creation, we are left with a difficult abstraction. This is true of course with any effort to directly describe some aspect of the nature of God. I refer the interested reader to chapter 1 of *The Nature and Character of God*, (C.Gaulden, eGen.co, Chambersburg, PA, 2016), for further discussion of such difficulties.

³ Hebrews 9:6-14 develops a clear sense of the futility of man-based redemptive actions. They would always be incomplete because as long as natural breath persisted in a human being, the "not-son" choice would be repeated.

⁴ Revelation 13:8 uses the phrase *"Lamb slain from the foundation of the earth"* in most translations. This is consistent with Revelation 5:6 in describing the Messiah. In other words, God the Father and God the Son knew before they began the acts of creation that the key creatures would need redemption in order to become sons of God and that the redemption would require the surety of the redemptive act, death, being provided by one not subject to the "not-son" choice. That one could be no other than the only begotten Son of God (God the Son), who was present when the Creation was brought into being. There is little dispute that the term "Lamb" in these passages refers to Jesus the Messiah. This redemption was as sure as the will of God because it was found in the will and design of the Godhead, which includes both the *guarantor* and the *guarantee* of the redemptive process. The process was foolproof because it involved the full participation of the Godhead in every one of its dimensions. Imperfection was to be corrected in this plan by a direct substitution of perfection for imperfection. Through this substitution, Jesus gives us power to become actualized sons of God (see Jn. 1:12).

⁵ Time as we know it apparently is not relevant in eternity, but was created as a fundamental component of The Creation. Its purpose seems to be to measure duration in a specifically delimited context. Because The Eternal, by nature and definition, is not delimited, a delimitation such as time would be unnecessary before The Creation came into being. In a simple way, time is introduced right off the bat in Genesis 1:5 to mark what we think of as days. Even the word "beginning" in Genesis 1:1 suggests this time phenomenon that had not existed before. If there is a corresponding marker similar to time in The Eternal, we do not know what it is and cannot learn it unless God reveals it.

⁶ See chapters 4-6 of *Birth of The Holy Nation, volume 1*, (C. Gaulden, eGenCo, Chambersburg, PA, 2015); for further discussion see also chapter 3 of *Nature and Character of God*, (C.Gaulden, eGen.co, Chambersburg, PA, 2016). Hebrews 1:3 is also useful.

⁷ The process of creation is really bringing something forth from nothing. The idea of making created substance from uncreated substance is a device for stating that fact. It is not that the quantity of uncreated substance is "used" in any way. The uncreated is not diminished in the acts of creation. There is no limit to the quantity of uncreated substance. There is a limit to created substance, both in time and quantity. When created substance ceases to be, it will in some sense "return" to the state of uncreatedness. The consequence will not be an increase in the quantity of the uncreated. It remains unaffected by the presence or absence of created substance. Because uncreated substance is unbounded it must contain, without any effect on itself one way or another, all of created substance. God and The Eternal are not far off. They are intimately close to us.

CHAPTER ONE

GETTING STARTED

In the beginning God created the heavens and the earth. The earth was formless and void, and darkness was over the surface of the deep, and the Spirit of God was moving over the surface of the waters. Then God said, "Let there be light"; and there was light. God saw that the light was good; and God separated the light from the darkness. God called the light day, and the darkness He called night. And there was evening and there was morning, one day (Genesis 1:1-5).

In the previous chapter we examined a very probable primary motivation for GOD to create The Creation. It is an inescapable conclusion that He already existed in some context before He "rolled up His sleeves" and began the processes that produced The Creation. The previous discussion implies that GOD could have decided not to create. According to scripture, though, He did, in fact, decide to create. At the risk of overstating the case, had He not decided to create, The Creation (including you and me) would not exist and this book would not be written. Even more importantly, scripture would not exist because there would be no need for it. These things being so, scripture has among its purposes an explanation of what GOD did and, to some extent, why He did what He did. The "what" of scripture is a bit more straightforward than the "why," but we may pursue aspects of both.[1]

The Bible's very first verse makes its initial intent clear. Scripture declares for itself that it is to begin with those things that have to do with the beginning of the acts of creation. In other words, before Genesis 1:1, there was nothing we could call "The Creation." The Creation, including all its components, simply did not exist before the dynamics of that verse. There was neither creation nor any component of creation. They did not exist in any sense except in the intentions of the already (and eternally) extant Creator. Whatever existed before Genesis 1:1 was not of created substance. GOD did not gather up a bunch of odd parts lying about in The Eternal and convert them into this new phenomenon. Among other things, one of scripture's main purposes is to capture the earliest moments of the existence of that which was to be created.

Neither in the Hebrew (Masoretic) nor the Greek (Septuagint or LXX) versions of Genesis 1:1 does a definite article appear before the word "beginning." In virtually every English translation of the Bible, however, the narrative begins thus: "In *the* beginning…" The word *the* does not appear in the Hebrew or Greek. If we remove the definite article, the resultant translation would read: "In beginning…" Let's not make too much of this, but there is a very special meaning that we should attach to the initial words of Genesis 1:1. I hope you will indulge me as I offer several tentative restatements of the verse. We might restate the first words of Genesis 1:1 in a number of other ways, such as:

"To get things started…"

"To begin with…"

"The first of all things was…"

If it be true, as we stated in the previous chapter, that GOD had a purpose that *required* The Creation, that purpose could not be fulfilled without The Creation. So, in order for GOD to bring about things that would arrive at the outcome determined by His purpose, He would have to start or begin the acts of creation. So scripture begins by saying,

"In the beginning GOD created…" This makes it clear that creation was not some set of spontaneous events. It couldn't have been. How could that which was created have come from that which was not created except there be some entity to direct the process? More cogently, it makes no sense to propose that something could accidentally come from nothing. GOD was the Actor who "got things started" by creating. He acted within the context of that which was not created in such a way that it gave rise to substance that was created. He acted on *that* and *this* came into being. As difficult as that is to understand, scripture really allows no other conclusion.

Before GOD acted, there was nothing that can be called The Creation. GOD acted by way of a verb we understand as "created," and what had not been came to be. It was not—and then He acted—and then it was. There was a point in time, as we think of it, that was *preceded by the absence of anything created*. Then there was a point in time when GOD acted. After that point in time, created things existed. As far as The Creation is concerned, it did not exist and then it existed because GOD acted in such a way as to cause it to exist. I don't think we can say we understand everything that is contained in the verb "created" as we find it in Genesis 1:1. At the very least it must convey some sense of amazing power. None of us is able to make something out of nothing. And then the sheer scale of GOD's creative actions is so awesome as to be incomprehensible to us in our finite capacity for understanding.

The Creation did not exist.

GOD created.

The Creation did exist.

We have already talked about "acts of creation" many times in this book so far. The noun "act" suggests action. Action is verbally based. We may think of an act or an action as some static observable phenomenon. At the same time, though, we understand that the act or action is really dynamic, that a change of some sort is occurring. For example, when we observe the winner of a foot race receiving congratulations

15

along with some token of victory, we know that the race has been conducted and that the winner changed location at a pace that exceeded that of the other racers. Simply put, the winner ran the fastest. When we consider the acts of creation our main interest is on the outcomes of those acts. In fact, when we say "acts of creation" we really mean the outcomes of the actions more than the actions themselves. But the actions that lead to the outcomes are also important, as they are the modalities which produce the outcome.

Genesis 1:1 strongly implies that the first "act of creation" happened instantly. GOD created "the heavens and the earth" in order to get things started. "The heavens and the earth" were the outcome of that first act of creation. GOD did not "make" them, as out of pre-existing matter; He "created" them out of nothing. Whatever GOD did that produced them was the set of actions. The statement implies that the whole thing – The Creation – happened quickly. There is no textual reason to believe that this took a long time. GOD just did it. He created, not with a set of instructions and a kit of materials, but *from nothing into something*. In some sense, He "created" by bringing into being a set of dimensions in which that which was created would be found while creating the substance that was to be found there. In other words, the verse seems to say that when He brought into being the *dimensions* of The Creation, those dimensions were simultaneously populated with the *stuff* of The Creation in full measure. It was all there; all the matter and all the energy along with their rules of order. The Creator did not have to wait on a shipment of parts. The rest of the narrative describes how He progressively brought order and specificity to the created substance.

The Verbs of Creation

We will get back to the narrative in just a bit. But before doing so, let's specify the "actions" that were involved in The Creation. *GOD was the* **Actor** *in every case*. He performed a deliberate action and His desired outcomes came to be, precisely as He intended. In fact, the Creator performed all His acts of creation in such a way that the entirety of what we call The Creation came into being fully formed and operational over a period of six days. This is our simple working paradigm.

> **GOD (the *Actor*) acted with some specific purpose.**
>
> **The *act* took a "form" in an operational sense (e.g. seeing is different from saying).**
>
> **The desired *outcome* came into being (e.g. "and there was light").**

In the creation narrative, GOD is both the sole Actor in and audience to the events. The actions that He undertook resulted in something new coming into being. Whatever it was did not exist, in any temporal sense anyway, until GOD acted; then it existed temporally from that time onward. The outcomes were purposes GOD had in the actions He undertook, and these actions suited the needs of His purposes in the things that came into being. Nothing GOD took action to bring into being existed before He brought it into being.

In listing the various verbs below, I will specify their most common form in the present tense (root verb, for our purposes). For example, I will use "create" even though the text says "created." Following the root verb will be a transliteration of the Hebrew verb as used in the text. For example, *barah* is a transliteration of the Hebrew word that means "create." The verbs typically appear in the third person, singular masculine form (e.g. He created). (The number indicates the Strong's number from the Hebrew section.) This is very reasonable because GOD is the Actor throughout. For our purposes, the term "creation narrative" covers the biblical material found in Genesis 1:1-2:4.[2]

- **CREATE:** (*barah*, 1254). The first action GOD undertook from within The Eternal, was to *create* the heavens and the earth. The heavens and the earth

17

have not always existed. GOD created them. From
the moment of that act of creation, the heavens
and the earth existed. The verb *barah* (create) appears six times in the creation narrative. Three of the
instances refer to specific actions, one is a redundant
use related to the third of the three main instances,
and the other two are general summary statements.
Certain aspects of this narrative are amplified later
in another chapter, particularly details related to the
bringing forth of man.

- **SAY:** (*amar,* 559) The second action GOD undertook
  was to *say,* "Let there be light."[3] The form of this verb
  in the text is past tense, "*said,*" because this all happened a long time ago. The verb, appearing ten times
  in the narrative, carries a clear sense of command.

- **SEE:** (*ra'ah,* 7200) This verb does not relate specifically to GOD's creative acts, but to the outcomes of those
  acts. As such, *ra'ah* reflects GOD's ongoing involvement. In a sense, He evaluated each of His actions,
  and the first step in that evaluation was to observe the
  outcome of those actions.[4] This verb appears seven
  times in the narrative.

- **CALL:** (*qara,* 7121) Like *ra'ah,* the Hebrew verb *qara*
  relates more to the outcome of the creative acts rather
  than the acts themselves. GOD took it upon Himself
  to "name" the outcomes of some of His acts. There
  was no one else around to do so. Thus it would have
  been hard to describe the outcomes without GOD *calling* them something. For example, try to describe light
  without *calling* it something. You get the idea. This
  verb appears five times in the narrative.

18

- **MAKE:** (*asah*, 6213) We first encounter this verb in Genesis 1:7, where GOD "made the expanse…" While this verb has some similarities to *barah* (create), *asah* refers more to converting something into something else than to bringing it into being from nothing. It is more like manufacturing than inventing. There remains a good bit of overlap in meaning between created and made, however. It appears that the verb references something already created being transformed in some manner into something else. Genesis 2:4 clarifies for us that "create" and "make" are separate but related ideas. The verb *asah* appears nine times in the narrative.

- **SEPARATE:** (*badal*, 914) This verb is subordinate to the verb "say" wherever it appears. In verse 6, GOD said (commanded) that some things be separated and then He separated them. The act of separation was the result of His command that it be so. The verb occurs three times in the narrative. The King James Version translates *badal* as "divide" rather than "separate."

- **GATHER:** (*qavah*, 6960) This verb is also subordinate. The Creator commanded that water be gathered. This happened without specification of an actor. We may asume that The Creation simply responded to the voice of GOD and did what it was told to do.[5] This verb appears only once in the narrative.

- **BLESS:** (*barak*, 1288) This verb appears three times in the creation narrative: once in reference to the sea creatures and the birds (1:22), once with reference to the man and woman (1:28), and once in reference to the seventh day (2:3). It is particularly significant for us to note that GOD specifically blessed the man and woman. In one sense, we could argue that all aspects of The Creation were blessed. However, the man and woman (humans) were specifically blessed in a manner far higher and greater than the rest of The Creation. This particularization probably means something for us today.

- **COMPLETE:** (*kalah*, 3615) This verb is used in the limited sense of termination. The time came when all the necessary acts of creation had been accomplished. As a verb of termination, *kalah* marks that particular temporal boundary. Thereafter, whatever was to occur would occur within the context of the already completed creation. This verb appears once only in the narrative.

There are a few other verbs within the creation narrative, but they refer generally to responses of various created entities to GOD's creative commands. They are the results of GOD commanding something He had made to act in a certain manner. For instance, verse 12 tells us that the earth and plants and trees "brought forth" various things in response to a command from GOD. I have not included those verbs in this discussion, but each is a response to GOD *saying* something. The following sections will focus on the relationships between GOD's actions and the various outcomes of those actions. The three most significant verbs are *create*, *say*, and *make*. Our analysis will focus primarily on these three.

GOD's Intention

In the previous chapter, we established that neither GOD nor eternity was diminished at all when the acts of creation took place. Rather, The Creation is in some sense a *dimension* of The Eternal and not separate from it. The Creation depends on GOD not only for its beginning but for its ongoing existence. The purposeful Creator sees to it that the ongoing dynamics and narrative of The Creation support that *purpose* for which He created it to begin with.

We established earlier that the primary purpose of the acts of creation likely was to bring into being entities that could be loved and had the potential of responding to that love in a positive and desired manner. In particular, GOD the Father would extend to those entities the love of a father, which we call *paternal love*. He would create these particular entities with the capacity to respond in the same manner as GOD the Son responded inside the Godhead. That responsive love we call *filial love*, the love of a son for a father.[6] In particular, His desire was that the "entity" He created, in all its instances, would emulate the Father just as the Son did within the Godhead. Fullness of this purpose, however, required that this same entity be capable of *not* responding as desired. Otherwise, the entity would be "robotic" rather than truly loving. Improper response of the entity to the Father's love would necessitate a divine intervention; what we call *redemption*.

GODS' purpose, then, was to produce sons who would love Him as the Son loved Him while being empowered to not do so if they so chose. However, exercising their power to choose in the negative would result in their falling away from the desired state of sonship. This, in turn, would require the provision of a plan for voluntary redemption to restore the fallen ones to their desired state of sonship. Otherwise, GOD risked having no sons. Redemption had to be foolproof, so He assured it with the life of THE Son, His "only begotten Son," who never required redemption.

"Morning and Evening"

Given the *power, purpose* and *motivation* of the Godhead, the acts of creation got underway by the determinate will of GOD. No other factor was necessary. GOD needed nothing but Himself to accomplish what He began in Genesis 1:1. So the work began.

It is important to note here that, generally speaking, modern science tells us that none of what was said above is true. The fundamental scientific explanation for the universe or *cosmos* (the physical aspects of what we are calling The Creation) is that the whole thing happened without the involvement of any conscious entity or purpose. To the naturalistic "keepers" of modern science, something that existed simply blew up because pressures within it became too great. In this view, the entire universe is the ongoing result of that explosion in which the various bits continue to travel away from one another because of the immense and inconceivable power of the explosion. Out of this basic theoretical idea the various natural sciences can be united into a single narrative. Among its elements is the idea that as the *great cosmic explosion* hurled matter and energy in every direction, various bodies developed and began natural histories of their own. Among those histories is that of the earth. That natural history requires an explanation of how life began and how the complex, thinking being known as *human* came to be. This is not the place to conduct a complete examination of all the elements that go into such thinking, but a couple of elements stand out. The first of these is the amazing *timespan* required from the explosion to the present timeframe. The second is the need for matter to change very *gradually* over time into more and more *complex* forms. In other words, over very long periods of time things became complex enough that "living" materials came into existence. Eventually, through even more complex mechanisms, humans came into being. The essential claim of this scientific view is that all these things took place without the involvement of any conscious or purposeful entity. Clearly, this view stands in stark contrast to the testimony of scripture.

Scripture presents the case that the existence of the physical cosmos is entirely dependent on the existence of the entity whom we call *The Creator*, who was quite *purposeful*. In this narrative The Creator caused everything to come into being and to take the forms He intended. A somewhat cursory but useful explanation of the initial sequence seems to be the purpose of the first chapter of Genesis. This narrative speaks to the issues of time, energy, and complexity of material in a very different manner than does science.

When we as humans think back on time we see it as something that is quite drawn out. This is largely due to the fact that we have been educated to think that way. The results of scientific man's *theoretical* examinations of what has been suggest very long timeframes and are presented as facts. This contributes to the sense of lengthy time periods leading up to today. The various sciences that produce these results have *methods* developed over time to keep them orderly. Their examinations must fit the scientific rules of order or they cannot be included in the body of knowledge that is furthered and protected by the science. This is perfectly understandable from the point of view of the scientists involved. At the same time, it is not required by scripture. Many, in fact, regard this as a weakness of scripture. However, it is not the purpose of scripture to conform to the rules of science. After all, GOD cannot be required to restrict Himself to those rules – He created them to partially govern His creation. The Genesis creation narrative is not, therefore, a scientific treatise. It is of another kind. Some propose that this makes scripture deficient. That proposition is not a scientifically honest one. Scripture is a narrative of a different kind than that of science; not deficient, just different.

The creation narrative presented in the first chapter of Genesis provides an important clue regarding time. A particular phrase, "there was evening and there was morning" (as translated in the NASB) appears six times in the chapter, and accompanies a series of six divisions of the work of creation. Each division of the work concludes with the phrase and is followed by the specification of a particular day to distinguish it from the others. For example, Genesis 1:5 ends with the sentence, "And there was evening and there was morning, one day." That particular sentence appears to be a bit ambiguous until you consider the other five similar statements. For example, Genesis 1:8 says, "And there was evening and there was morning, a second day." The Hebrew text of verse 5 really says, "day one." Verse 8 literally reads, "day second," and so forth in verses 13, 19, 23, and 31. The days are distinguished from one another in an ordered sequence and correspond to increasingly complex outcomes. In the table below, the verses column refers to the verses in Genesis chapter 1 in which the relevant material is recorded.

FOCUS	DAY	VERSES
Matter and light (energy)	Day One	1-5
Earth and "else" distinction	Second Day	6-8
Dry land, seas, and vegetation	Third Day	9-13
Heavenly bodies and seasonal forces	Fourth Day	14-19
Airborne and waterborne animate creatures	Fifth Day	20-23
Land-based animals and "man"	Sixth Day	24-31

Generally, the Genesis narrative presents the unfolding of the acts of creation in a sequence of increasing complexity reaching its pinnacle on the sixth day of the creation cycle. This creative work does not require billions of years. The plain sense of the text states that it took six days, each day resulting in some finished state that gave rise to the work of the next day.

With God

Let's examine the "days" a bit more closely. More specifically, let's examine the concept of a "day" more closely. The text of Genesis 1 presents the acts of creation occurring over six periods of time we normally think of in terms of 24 hours each. There is little room to think otherwise insofar as the actual text is concerned. There are, though, some problems in considering the acts of creation in too simplistic a manner. God was creating an entirely new context called The Creation. As far as we know, there were no witnesses to the events of that week except the Godhead. It is highly likely that not even angels were present, as they were created after The Creation was at least partially "completed" in its final form. That final form was the one into which the first man was placed at the time of his creation. Scripture states that time does not mean the same thing to God as it does to us (2 Peter 3:8). Of course it doesn't. He *created* time and is not bound by it, while our lives and perceptions while on earth are governed by it.

Some want to help GOD out and suggest that the various days of the creation narrative refer to thousand-year increments per Peter. This line of thought often goes on to remove the equivalency that Peter allegorically alludes to so that a thousand years morphs in our thinking to billions of years without our awareness that we have done that. It may be that the six days of creation refer to very long timeframes as this theory suggests. However that is not necessary and seems contrary to the plain sense of the passage. That apparent difficulty is the one in which we need some clarity. It is not likely that we can totally resolve the apparent difficulties, but we can at least place them in some clarity that is better than a superficial reading mixed with political motivation can accomplish.

The primary problem with the rather loose interpretive method described in the previous paragraph lies in the precision of the language of Genesis. Six times in chapter 1 it specifies that an "evening" and a "morning" were a day. Evening and morning may mean something different to GOD than they do to us, but scripture makes no specification one way or the other in the matter. The language suggests these were literal days as we commonly define them, something like 24-hour periods of time.[7]

It is not the purpose of this work to get into a heated argument regarding the matter of 24-hour days in Genesis 1. Our purpose is to get at the reasonableness of a literal reading of the narrative. It often seems unreasonable to assert this standard day as the proper interpretation, but what is the motive for that argument? It seems the motive may be to "give GOD a break." After all, the argument implies, it would take a very long time for such things to occur. That would be true in the standard scientific model. But would an omnipotent Creator require long periods of time? Could He complete the various stages of the creation work in standard days? If we affirm that He could do so, can we accept the idea that He would do so? The challenge here is to decide whether we *can* believe the biblical record regarding the time it took for The Creation to come into its full order. I understand that scientific theory argues a very different set of conclusions based on its rules of evidence. This is not an argument against what scientists have concluded in their theories in regard to time in the universe. The question regards the capacities of GOD. The biblical record suggests a period of six literal days for the entire creation cycle to occur. I leave it to the reader to consider the main question in this paragraph: *could* GOD do the whole thing in six days? Is GOD bound by the results of scientific observation, which is bound by the rules of science?

Finally, at Mt. Sinai the Israelites were instructed in the matter. Regarding the Sabbath, GOD instructed them concerning the structure of a work week (Ex. 20:9-11). In the eleventh verse the text strongly implies equivalency in the days under discussion. The Sabbath, or seventh day, came after the six days of creation. The text is not fully definitive, but the implication is strong that the day periods are equivalent.

On the other hand, let's remember that **GOD *was the only witness*** to what He was doing.[8] Furthermore, let's remember that He even created time as we think of it. Time serves very practical purposes in the physical universe. Its presence is also implied in the heavens, which are not physical. For example, the book of Revelation contains quite a bit of information regarding temporal sequences of events and even mentions one period of 1000 years (Rev. 20:2-3). Furthermore, Genesis 1:5 implies the simultaneous creation of time with the physical universe when it says "there was evening and there was morning." As we know, the sun and moon were not created until the fourth day, and they function to mark day and night as their most obvious activity. Nonetheless, the text specifies something like this on the first day.

GOD and His actions are not time delimited. He may act completely outside any context we can imagine with no time related constraints on His actions. So, GOD did not have to take time into consideration when He began the acts of creation. On the other hand, He would eventually communicate the acts and their sequence to us. Perhaps He narrated the acts of creation to Adam, who passed them on to his son in time. We do not know that. We should not suppose, however, that the recording of the acts was necessary within the Godhead, the only witness to the acts themselves. We know that on the first day of creating, He chose to address The Creation (in the absence of sentient creatures) orally when He issued His first command. The man was not yet created. It is not clear the angels had been created yet. So GOD must have addressed Himself and the non-sentient creation. In the absence of a recording device, He must then have intended that we would "hear" the command. In fact, throughout the week of the acts of creation, He made a number of announcements and issued a number of commands. He remembered them and communicated them to us. In a sense, we have only His word for what transpired. I hope we all agree that is adequate. So, for example, GOD said, "Let there be light" (Gen. 1:3). He then purposefully remembered doing that and communicated it to us at the time of His choosing. In so doing, He made no error, nor did He practice any deceit. However, He might well have provided us with that information in terms that we could understand but which were irrelevant to Him.

There can be no reasonable doubt that in matters of such scale and importance, many of the purposes of GOD were being initiated at once, so to speak, at least in any sense we can understand. In this analysis, we have deliberately focused on the physical aspects of these *cosmological* events. There are many spiritual aspects as well. I use the term *cosmological* to refer to the physical universe, not spiritual realities. At the moment creation began to occur, there was the need to birth the physical out of the spiritual. In a setting like that, it must be true that the transition spawned results in both contexts. As Sam Soleyn has demonstrated,[9] it must be true that GOD ushered in The Creation from The Eternal in both contexts simultaneously. For example, John speaks to us very forthrightly about the Light (Jn. 1:4-9). He states that JESUS was the Light that "shines in the darkness" (Jn. 1:5). That is a spiritual phenomenon. At the same time, light was said to separate day from night, well in advance of the creation of the sun and moon, whose first physical function is just that (Gen. 1:14). In both contexts, light reveals the works of GOD.

Given what we just said about GOD's ability to act entirely outside time, He chose to take "six days" to enact the acts of creation. At one level, that is astounding. To have done all He did in only six days was quite a feat. In fact, to have done it at all was amazing. However all that worked out, GOD chose to include time somehow in His acts. So the first day preceded the second day and so forth. As we saw earlier, there was a logical "rolling out" of the products of His acts. On the first day, however, He chose to create the heavens and the earth and to leave the earth in an essentially chaotic state. Into that environment He spoke and introduced light. Then, *in the light of the Light,* order began to come into the brand new creation. Some period of time then passed before He acted again. The passage describes epistemological facts within the frame of the acts of creation. Only GOD, who can perfectly well act outside time, was a witness to how time acted in that setting. That same GOD chose to preserve for us the knowledge of the time involved insofar as the temporal sequencing of His various acts and pronouncements.

Evening and Morning

If there was evening and morning on the first day, as the text states, there must be some meaning to them. Our only context is temporal in this case because there was no sunrise or sunset. So why might the term be present? Who said so anyway? We have already established that GOD "authored" and preserved the accounts of those first several days. No one else was present. He preserved the information so that someday, somehow, He could communicate the record to someone. At the time He chose to communicate the information to someone, we can rest assured it was accurate information. GOD knew what He was doing and we cannot suppose He was communicating untruth when the time came for the record of His doings to be captured for us.

There are some subsidiary questions beyond the scope of this work. It is not our purpose to answer all those questions. Our subject matter is the *purpose* of creation, not its *mechanics*. It may be that the various "day" summary statements refer to some enormous timeframes, but the language does not suggest that, and GOD does not seem to need really long timeframes in which to allow things to develop as they will. Long timeframes suit the idea that things would "evolve" in a leisurely manner. Such a thing may be, but does GOD need to just permit things to evolve as they will? Or can He direct how things will be? It seems He could and would direct how things develop if He has a purpose in it to begin with. That is one of the premises under which we are operating in pursuing this study.

First Actions

The Genesis narrative begins with a statement we translate as, "In the beginning God created the heavens and the earth" (Gen. 1:1). We were not given the definition of the word "create," but generally we know that it has to do with bringing something into being. How He brought it into being is the description of the verb "create." For example, did He reach into some extra-cosmic bag of materials and pull out a handful of some extra-cosmic material and turn it into the stuff of creation? We simply don't know. There were no witnesses to the very first act of creation (making heavens and earth come into being), so there is no testimony in terms of a visual description of the event.

Actually, there were witnesses, in a sense. The Godhead was fully aware of what the Godhead was doing as the acts of creation began to be undertaken. John 1:3, 10 specify that one known as "the Word" was active in the work of creation. We understand that passage to refer to GOD the Son. If it be so that He is the Word, then He was an active participant, not just a witness to the acts of creation. That is the specific testimony of John. Perhaps the Godhead placed the actual work of creation in the hands of the Word (GOD the Son). If that is so, and John strongly implies it, then there might be other traces of some sort of a division of labor within the Godhead as The Creation came into being. Genesis 1:2 implies exactly that. Looking at the two passages in tandem, we might conclude that GOD the Son was busy doing whatever creating was and the Spirit of GOD was in attendance in some manner; the Spirit was the witness.

The language changes a bit in Genesis 1:3: "Then God said…" The word "said" comes from the verb "say," which is not the same thing as "create." There may be some minimal semantic overlap between the two verbs, but very little. This, then, was a different thing than what occurred in verse 1. When GOD *spoke* the light into being, He seems to have been doing something different from what He did when He *created* the matter and space of The Creation. Let's remain cognizant of the fact that the folks who gave us the text of this narrative might just have been using a variety of verbs to keep the narrative interesting, but that does not seem to be the case at all. Furthermore, we may inquire as to whom He spoke. Obviously, He spoke to Himself and then captured that fact for us.

GOD had something different in mind when He *created* matter and space than when He *spoke* light into being. Matter (and the space that separates matter into discrete increments) performs certain functions in The Creation, and light performs other functions. They are of different kind. Therefore, the acts that brought each into being could well be of different kind. GOD did *this* to create matter and He did *that* to bring forth light. *This* and *that* are different from one another in the results produced; they are complementary, not identical. For example, identifiable light sources would later come into being that would help rule what happened in the material world. Initially, though, light came into being in The Creation because The Light "appeared" in The Creation. GOD the Son appeared here because GOD the Father stated that it should be so.

"The Surface of the Waters"

The apparent meanings of subsequent sections of the creation narrative suggest that the matter that GOD created on Day One (the first day) was fairly undifferentiated in its nature. Later that week, as the acts progressed, greater and greater differentiation occurred. But, at first, there was not a lot of differentiation.

There does, however, appear to be an initial differentiation between what we call earth, in the sense of dry surface and water. They came forth at the same time (the "created" verb) but in different *kind*. On the third day these different *kinds* would come to be separated into coherent areas on the earth (Gen. 1:9).

Coincidentally, light was not differentiated at that time as far as we can discern from the text. GOD simply brought forth light without any source other than Himself. It was to be the fourth day before He created other light sources (Gen. 1:14). In fact, the text implies He did distinguish between light and dark on Day One. Can we imagine a universe in which light and darkness actually coexisted in a way in which we could not tell them apart? There are some theological implications inherent in that question. Remember that JESUS was even called "the Light" (Jn. 1:9). John 1:5 does provide salience to the distinction between the two phenomena, by the way. The Creator did not leave all that unaddressed, though. He did in fact *separate* light from dark during the day in which light came into being. Again, we can hardly imagine that it would be otherwise, but that is what we have always known and we explain such things in ways that are consistent with our experience with them.

Day One (Sunday, Abib 1) Genesis 1:1-5

As far as we know, days and other markers of time passage do not exist in the Eternal. If they did, we could specify that on one Saturday evening, at a time shortly after sundown, GOD suddenly created the heavens and the earth. Specifically, He created solid matter, water, and spatial separation between them. Solid stuff and water were created and simultaneously hung in "space" all at the same time. Did this take hours or minutes or only moments, or was it instantaneous? However long it took, it all fit into a timeframe that was less than half a day long insofar as the biblical text is concerned.[10]

Okay, what's the Saturday night business? The day on which this all took place was called Day One. This is the first day of the Jewish week to this day. It is the day we call Sunday. In the Jewish way of seeing things (biblically-based, by the way), the day begins at sundown, not at sunrise or midnight. So it was, actually would come to be, that this first work of creation took place as Day One began. In point of fact, Day One began to be when these first acts of creation began. As every day begins at sundown, Day One began at sundown. In the historical and modern Jewish reckoning of things, Day One begins right after sundown of a *Shabat* (Saturday). So at sundown of a Saturday that never existed, GOD got started. In the first half of that day He made solid matter, water, space, and time. Darkness was a property of the matter and water that He made.[11] We may posit that GOD did not create dark. It was only a state that existed before He brought forth light. In fact, we generally think of darkness as the absence of light. Interestingly, the light that GOD spoke into being on Day One seems to correspond well with the Light found in The Eternal.

When He spoke light into being it immediately impacted the darkness that was a property of what He had created earlier that day. After that, mostly undifferentiated matter[12] and undifferentiated light existed side-by-side for a while, more or less independently. The Second Day was given over almost entirely to bringing order to that which had been created during Day One. Matter was there subject to the ongoing work of GOD. Light apparently came and went in a cycle called "evening and morning." As the week of creation passed, GOD brought high levels of differentiation of matter into being. He also brought into being various *natural* sources of light, as well as specific relationships between matter and light.

Space was not the only device GOD put in place to govern how various forms of matter in The Creation related to one another. He also brought gravity into being to work with space to keep the various created entities in proper relationship to one another. So space, time, and gravity were all created as properties that GOD produced to cause The Creation to exist in some kind of order. Our Father is, after all, an orderly GOD.

What do we have? On Day One, GOD *created* water[13] and other undifferentiated matter, and whatever is meant by the term "heavens."

It is possible that water was the only matter present, but, as we discussed, that is not likely and is inconsistent with the plain sense of the text. Later that day, He *spoke* light into being. Then He clearly distinguished light from darkness. However, before He separated them, He evaluated light and found that it was good.[14] In the subsequent days, He would go through the processes of making many things from undifferentiated matter. He would also create sources of light. But light was already good from His viewpoint. On the subsequent days He was to see that the day's work product was good. But on Day One, it was light that received His specific approval (see 1 Jn. 1:5). We may say that light was the pinnacle achievement of Day One and provides a scriptural preview of the One who was to come to show man the way to the Father through the love mechanism. The light was created, in a sense, but The Light also showed up in response to the voice of GOD emanating from the Godhead.

It is important to note that chaos and darkness would have continued to be the states in which these things co-existed, but GOD brought necessary *order* into the mix as well.[15] Out of His own being He granted the authority necessary for space, gravity, and time to begin to govern the components of The Creation. When He gave light the power to "overcome" darkness, He separated the two. Again, this separation contributes to our understanding of the order that governs The Creation in an overall sense.

Day One came to an end, and all these things were in place. GOD had set the stage for the rest of the work He had set for Himself. As we shall see, over the next five days GOD would develop the initial creation into its marvelous complexity with His future sons at its apex.

---

[1] Second Timothy 3:16 tells us that scripture can be used in a variety of ways. It must, therefore, have a variety of purposes. Just as we have declared that GOD is purposeful in His acts of creation, so we declare that scripture is given by GOD to us with His purposes in mind. One of the purposes of scripture is to reveal to us what GOD wanted and was doing at the time of initial creation.

[2] Wiseman makes a strong case that Genesis was compiled from a group of documents that were passed down over time and came into the care of the compiler, assumed to be Moses. P. J. Wiseman, *Ancient Records and the Structure of Genesis*, (Nashville: Thomas Nelson Publishers, 1985). The lack of any other-witnesses argues that GOD dictated the earliest materials to someone. Arguably, that someone was Adam, but there are several other candidates. Whoever received the dictations, it seems clear that GOD wanted an accurate record to be kept because He desired that we be informed of His labors. And He is certainly capable of ensuring the accuracy of the records.

[3] Between the first instance of "create" and the first instance of "say" is the statement about the Spirit of GOD "hovering." This may be as much a statement of a state of being as of an action. I acknowledge the hovering had a purpose, but have not included it in this analysis because it had no apparent outcome in and of itself. Deeper analysis of this would be a matter of theological discourse that is outside our current discussion.

[4] This verb helps us understand GOD's appraisal through the use of a verb we can relate to. In this instance, thinking of GOD in anthropomorphic (human-like) terms is appropriate. In fact, the entire verbal presentation of the creation cycle requires that we think anthropomorphically because we cannot comprehend GOD in a manner that actually describes Him. Hence, we will mentally use forms we can understand.

[5] By implication, the water was initially "un-gathered." The command for the waters to be gathered resulted in a greater order in the state of things in the earth. Un-gathered water must be less orderly than gathered water. The command specifies no actor. Perhaps The Creation itself responded to the command. Certainly, The Creation currently longs for the return of order (see Rom. 8:19-22). By this we argue that the entropic (chaotic) creation has a primal need to be restored to its most orderly state, that which it had just after the cessation of the acts of creation.

[6] A fairly detailed discussion of *paternal love* and *filial love* can be found in the first six chapters of C. Gaulden, *Birth of the Holy Nation, volume 1*, (Chambersburg: eGenCo, 2015). For the moment, suffice it to say that paternal love is always first and filial love is a response to paternal love. GOD the Father and GOD the Son and their relationship are the first and most perfect exemplars of the nature of that love pair. Paternal love originates in a father and finds a son as its object. Filial love originates in a son and is a response in which the father is the object.

[7] Interestingly, the order of the day parts is evening then morning. Mostly, we order our day parts as morning (beginning at midnight) then evening. This has to do with lunar versus solar reckoning. To the Hebrew (and many other peoples in the world), the day begins with the time of seeing the moon and stars, which is about sunset. The day begins when the moon begins to be the "ruling light" and continues until about the same time the next day. This is not scientific. It is a matter of definition, not detail. See Genesis 1:14-19, Day Four. Of course, we will often see the moon during daylight hours, but it is "subordinate" to the sun in its luminary impact on the dark. On Day One, GOD used the term "evening and morning" to delimit a period even though the luminary bodies were not yet created. This gets into the matter of Light and light.

[8] I am deeply indebted to Sam Soleyn for his understanding and teaching on this matter. The implications of this statement are very significant. If GOD was the only conscious entity present at the time, it must be He who provided the details to someone (Adam?) after The Creation was finished. Our traditions often ascribe the writing of the book of Genesis to Moses. The question has to do with how Moses constructed that history so long after it had occurred. Whether Adam or Moses or someone else was the "writer," he needed access to information about the earliest moments. GOD must have dictated that information in some manner. If the information came directly from GOD, it must be accurate.

[9] See www.soleyn.com/media-download. The relevant recording is labeled "Session 2 – ASOM Santiago DR 2016." The date of the recording is December 5, 2016.

---

[10] The text does not provide us with any hint at timeframes of billions of years, nor would they be necessary for a God of unlimited powers. Science requires the very long timeframes because it cannot consider that there is a purpose or even consciousness behind these acts. To science they are simply a cascade occurring over extremely long times. This is required for the theory of singularity to work. At the same time, it appears that time was not a property to be found in The Eternal. That being so, time would really mean nothing at the first instants of creation. However, God presented the information to us as He did, and that implies actual days. Efforts to resolve this have been inconclusive. We do not need to take up for science in the matter. This work is an analysis of textual content and should not be used to solve the arguments over such ideas as gaps in the Bible.

[11] The entire flavor of scripture is that there is no darkness in The Eternal. Revelation 22, for example, emphasizes this in its description of the New Jerusalem. Life and light are equated in the discussion of Jesus' description in John 1. See also 1 John 1:5.

[12] Matter was not entirely undifferentiated. At a minimum, solid matter was differentiated from water at the outset. The only other alternative conclusion for us is that water is the only matter that was created at the beginning. This is at odds with the language of Genesis 1:1 unless even the earth was only water at first. In that case, the act of gathering water so land could appear in verse 9 was an act in which two things happened: water was contained and land was created. Again, that seems unlikely. The more likely case is that water was created as a differentiated form of matter and that all other matter was created in undifferentiated fashion. Initially, in this model, water covered all the undifferentiated matter. Subsequently, particularly on the Second Day, matter other than water began to be differentiated as well.

[13] Scripture often refers to water in a spiritual context that parallels its physical nature and functions. This may well be the case in the early passages of Genesis. At the same time, it seems clear that water was also being spoken of in a natural sense. In the plain sense of the passage, water covered things and thereby obscured them until it was brought into order. In that sense, water gave the appearance of formlessness to the earth. Early on, "water" might have been used to refer to the formlessness of space as well.

[14] We almost must infer darkness had not been present in The Eternal. When the very first acts of creation were undertaken, it soon became necessary to require that light be brought into The Creation so that it could experience light. It is very tempting to propose that this was at once both physical and spiritual and that it was the coming of Light (God the Son, see John 1) that brought light as a physical phenomenon. In this scenario, the Godhead created the heavens and the earth. Then God the Father spoke and God the Son entered the new creation and carried out the rest of the acts of creation. Darkness had not previously existed as a phenomenon; there had been no lack of light in The Eternal.

[15] Order is imposed by some entity that has the authority and power to require that it be so. Authority is one of the basic properties or characteristics of God discussed in C. Gaulden, *The Nature and Character of God*, (Chambersburg: eGenCo, 2016). All authority originates in God. The implementation of any authority will result in some form of order when the entity issuing authority possesses the requisite power. God's omnipotence is the conduit through which the authority of God was released to bring order into the new creation. In a sense, we might say that God "released" space, gravity, and time as forms of His authority into The Creation as He created it. Separateness is a subset of space.

CHAPTER TWO

HEAVENS AND ANGELS

While "the heavens" are not the subject of this book, they are nevertheless a worthy and interesting subject. For that reason, let's digress a bit and examine some basic information found in scripture regarding the heavens. While we're at it, we will also consider "angels" because of their importance to mankind. Neither of these are core topics for us, but they do provide part of the overall backdrop of scripture that can help us in our understanding of the topic at hand. Also, the fallen angel Satan figures early and prominently in the story of Adam and Eve, particularly as the catalyst to their downfall. To some extent, the placement of this material at this point in the book is arbitrary. At the same time, however, this information will prove useful when we come to the garden of Eden material.

The Bible is a book compiled for the sake of mankind so we can come to some understanding of the relationship between GOD and The Creation, which is the setting in which that relationship and its dynamics occur. This is true, at least, insofar as humans are concerned. According to the best information we have, the heavens did not exist prior to the acts of creation. This appears to be the only reasonable inference from Genesis 1:1: "In the beginning God created the heavens and the earth."

The Heavens did not exist before The Creation

Because The Creation includes both the heavens and the earth, the heavens are, of necessity, a subset of The Creation. We may view it in the following manner. The earth is a component of The Creation. If we consider The Creation in such a manner as to exclude either the earth or the heavens from the discussion, we will be examining something less than the totality of The Creation. Another way of viewing this statement is additively:

The Creation consists of The Earth plus The Heavens

It is fairly easy for us to agree on what we mean when we say "the earth." We might quibble in a minor way as to whether or not to include the atmosphere that surrounds the earth in our definition, but a fairly non-contentious agreement will settle the definition fairly well. For our purposes, we will include the atmosphere because of its constant accompaniment of the earth, and because of the functions it performs to protect the earth and its inhabitants from the hazards of "outer" space.

Therefore, whatever The Heavens are, they are not included when we refer to The Earth except by the automatic exclusion of The Heavens from The Earth. "The Earth" is one set of phenomena and "The Heavens" is another set of phenomena. This is not to suggest that there is some sort of absolute exclusion of all entities found in the heavens from the earth or vice-versa,[1] but to point out that fundamentally, these two subsets of The Creation are not the same. They are readily distinguishable from one another. That said, I propose that the functions of the heavens are not all carried out in the earth. They may well be necessary for *proper* functioning of the earth, but are operationalized in the heavens. The angels of Jacob's dream were probably not just traveling back and forth. More likely, they were performing acts in the earth that were determined and empowered in the heavens. The purposes behind their ascending and descending have implications beyond the scope of this work.

Heaven or Heavens

Having concluded that "the earth" and "the heavens" are distinct, non-identical phenomena, let's move on to another matter. The earth is a singular phenomenon. There could be multiple earths, but scripture suggests there is only one. Genesis 1:1 is not ambiguous as to the number of entities it calls "earth." To a degree, with respect to the conclusions we reach regarding the number of earths, the scriptural text suggests the earth is a unique phenomenon. I understand scientific speculation suggests other similar places *might* exist, but the biblical text adds nothing to that speculation.

When it comes to "the heavens," though, we confront a different situation. In every case in which it occurs, the Hebrew word is plural. Some scholars suggest this is a linguistic quirk and that the word is singular but in a plural form. That particular argument needs closer examination.

The basic question is simple: if the biblical text gives evidence of only one phenomenon called "the heavens," it is reasonable to reduce the term to "heaven." If, on the other hand, there is no clear evidence of the singularity of the "heaven" phenomenon, then to suggest that the Hebrew word, although plural in form, is intended to be understood as referring to a singularity would appear to be misleading, however well-intentioned. There may be cases in scripture in which the text clearly specifies a single phenomenon, but in the absence of such clarity we risk creating ambiguity by insisting a word means something different than what it plainly says. Furthermore, if there are multiple heavens, to refer to any one of them would require specificity, but to refer to them all simultaneously would require only the one plural word.

By contrast, the Greek text of the New Testament uses only a singular word for the same phenomenon. A plural form is not used in the NT. It turns out this is also the case in the Septuagint (LXX). In Genesis 1:1, LXX uses the singular word for heaven. So we are left with a bit of a conundrum. Greek texts use the singular form exclusively and Hebrew texts use the plural form exclusively. This may at first appear to be a matter of importance only to academics, but we are trying to establish what GOD created on the first day of the creative acts. In fact, the first thing mentioned in the text among the products of GOD's creative activity is "the heavens." This event is specified before the creation of the earth even if the two acts were in some sense simultaneous. In that case, "the heavens" were created at the same time as "the earth." Whether there is more than one heaven, then, is an important matter.

GOD's "Home"

Before we get to that however, let's deal with the incomprehensible yet essential fact that while the heavens are *created*, GOD is *not created*. Or rather, He is *uncreated*. He instructed the prophet Isaiah in this matter.[2] The instruction, while poetic in form, is fairly specific. In essence, He told Isaiah that "the heavens" (plural) are merely a seat to Him–specifically, a throne. If the heavens are only a throne for Him, how then could a man contemplate building an actual house for Him? GOD even specifically reiterated for Isaiah that He had made the heavens and the earth.

GOD *was not homeless* prior to the act of creating the heavens. He has not disclosed much about His living conditions before He created the heavens, but we can be sure He was not a homeless vagabond of some sort. That being the case, we should not fall into the trap of thinking that GOD "lives" in heaven or the heavens. In much of our casual, popular theology we say that GOD lives in heaven. According to scripture, this simply is not true. GOD does not "live" in the heavens and He did not create them as a home for Himself. We do see a throne in the heavens in the context of the revelations that John received in a vision while in exile on the island of Patmos.[3] A throne is a place from which a monarch rules, but it is not the monarch's home even if it sits in the monarch's home. This is perfectly consistent with GOD's admonition in Isaiah 66:1-2.

**GOD does not live in heaven or The Heavens;
they are but a throne room.**

Does It Matter?

One day JESUS' disciples requested that He teach them to pray.[4] In honoring their request, He introduced a very interesting idea. He taught them that it was desirable that matters in the earth be as they were in heaven. In particular, He stated that GOD's will was accurately honored in heaven. Wherever GOD resides, He is the absolute sovereign and there is no question concerning adherence to His will. His residence there makes the matter moot. By implication, that was not the case on earth, and even in heaven it was an observable fact that His will was done rather than being moot. We should, according to JESUS, beseech the Father that He intervene in some manner so that adherence to His will in the earth would come to be as important and accurate as it is in heaven.

Heaven (or the heavens), then, was notable for this difference from the earth at the time JESUS was instructing His disciples. Without fanfare, JESUS taught them that the will of GOD was done in heaven. At the same time, He taught them to desire (and pray) that the will of GOD be done in the earth also, and to the same degree. A condition existed in heaven that was superior to its corollary in the earth, but the prayer asked that an equivalency be established between the two.

So yes, it matters. Whatever other purposes the heavens might serve in The Creation, they serve as a standard for measuring adherence to the will of GOD. The question for us is whether we can look to the heavens for guidance concerning the will of GOD, or at least in the matter of honoring His will with adherence to the implied standards of His will.

One Heaven?

We still haven't settled on whether there is simply "heaven" or whether The Creation contains multiple entities called "the heavens." On one occasion, JESUS stated He had seen "*Satan fall from heaven like lightning*" (Lk. 10:18). At some time or other, JESUS had witnessed an event in which Satan was in a heavenly realm[5] and for some reason fell from that realm. Another passage makes it clear that Satan did not fall to earth (yet another realm) at that time. Rather, he was in a heavenly realm and fell from there to some other realm that was not earth. Because The Creation consists of "heavens" and "the earth," according to the Genesis text, we might posit the provisional conclusion that when Satan fell, he fell from one heaven to another heaven. If this conclusion proves accurate, then at least two heavens were created.

This passage must be distinct from Revelation 12:9, which prophesies that Satan will be cast down to the earth.[6] This is a specific future event, not the same one Jesus referred to in the Gospel of Luke. In the first event, Satan fell (past tense). In the second, he will be (future tense) "thrown down." In this event, Satan is to be forced out of one heaven or another onto the earth.

Yet another passage suggests there are at least three heavens. Paul "knew" a man who was "caught up to the third heaven" (2 Cor. 12:2). Paul was bearing witness to the fact that the man he knew was "caught up" to a specific entity that he called the "third heaven." If there is a *third* heaven, logically there must be at least two other heavens. It is certainly reasonable to assume, based on these facts, that GOD created *at least three heavens* at or close to the same time He created the earth.

Three Heavens?

If all of this is true and consistent with scripture (and I believe it is), then GOD created at least three heavens at the same time He created the earth. This is consistent with the use of the plural "heavens" in Genesis 1:1 But this begs the question: why three heavens? Wouldn't one be enough? Certainly, what we commonly think of as heaven is quite awesome. It makes us feel the earth is quite small when compared to the expanse of the heavens. And somewhere on the far side of heaven, in this theology, is where GOD lives and where we will all go someday.

The prospect of multiple heavens raises additional questions as well. How can we distinguish one heaven from another? How are they similar to each other? How are they different? What is their purpose? These are unanswerable questions by any means available to us. We can, however, make some observations about them, which will enable us, to a limited extent, to reflect on the differences between them.

Third Heaven

Let's begin with the third heaven (Third Heaven), which is arguably the highest heaven. This heaven is not visible to us. It does not have dimensionality as we think of such on the earth. As a created realm, however, it must have some form of dimensionality. Certainly it begins and ends in some time-delimited dimensionality, even if we cannot think in terms of length and width. Paul spoke very explicitly about Third Heaven (see 2 Cor. 12:2-4). In one notable expression, he described it as a place where he "*heard inexpressible words, which a man is not permitted to speak*" (2 Cor. 12:4). By the way, Paul mentions Paradise in the same context. Is he implying that Paradise is the same thing as Third Heaven?

We already saw that John went into a heaven in which was the throne of GOD. (see Rev. 4:1-2). The throne was the central focus of everything John saw and every action that took place following his arrival. This is probably the same heaven where Isaiah received his instructions and Paul heard the "inexpressible words." Visitations to (or visions of) that heaven, on the part of humans, seem to be rather rare events. We are tempted to believe that this heaven is the one from which Daniel received a messenger who brought information to him, some of which Daniel was not permitted to share with us in his writings.[7]

Please bear with me as I present the possibility that it was in this realm,[8] the third heaven, where Satan appeared among the sons of GOD.[9] This seems quite reasonable to me because even if Satan was not a resident in Third Heaven at the time, he might still have had access as GOD saw fit. Hence, from his probable place in the second heaven (see below) he might be able to ascend to Third Heaven on certain occasions, including the two instances recorded in the book of Job.

This is reasonable as he was first a resident of Third Heaven and was in some sense existentially compatible with it.[10]

Taking these portions of scripture together, we can construct a partial description of the realm we are calling Third Heaven. This realm might well be the place GOD constructed within The Creation from which His absolute will and rule are expressed to The Creation and those who dwell in it. The throne in Third Heaven would become the locus through which the relevant aspects of The Eternal came to The Creation. Its focal point is a throne. From that throne, angels receive instruction that is to be carried out in the "lower" realms, including the earth. In this realm, Third Heaven, the most wonderful things in The Creation are to be found. In this realm, the will of GOD is the absolute status of all things. The few human visitors who have reported to us concerning what they know of that realm were constrained in certain ways from providing a full description because things there are too wonderful to be revealed to us prematurely.

One may interpret that the messenger sent to Daniel (Dan. 10:12) came forth from Third Heaven as a result of Daniel's pleas. He was detained in the second heaven (see below) for a time until Michael came from Third Heaven to finish that struggle while the first angel finished his journey of revelation to Daniel. I realize this is an interpretation that doesn't sit well with most of our theologies, but it seems to me a good fit to the textual material at hand.

Second Heaven

We have the least evidence concerning the second heaven (Second Heaven). It seems reasonable to assume that it was created and does exist because the numerical sequence is: one, two, three. Having only a third heaven makes no sense. If there is such a realm, and if Genesis 1 is correct, it is fairly easy to discuss a first heaven. The second heaven must exist simply from an epistemological perspective. But there is more.

As we have seen, Satan fell, at some time in the past, from (a) heaven (Lk. 10:18) to some other realm. That realm was not the earth.

This is clear from the fact that his exile to the earth is yet to come (Rev. 12:9). The heaven from which he fell is one realm. The earth to which he is to be exiled is yet a separate realm. There must be an intermediate realm to which he fell in the first instance. One may argue that the intermediate realm is the natural universe. That seems unlikely because the earth and the natural universe are so closely associated. In fact, the realm we call earth is actually a component, or subset of the physical universe.[11] Momentarily, we will consider that the physical universe is the first heaven plus the earth.

Even after his fall from some realm (heaven) to another realm (heaven), Satan remains busy. JESUS speaks of Satan as a murderer, a liar, and the father of lies (Jn. 8:44). We have seen that Satan appeared before GOD to request permission to torment Job (Job 1:6; 2:1). He personally saw to the temptation of JESUS in the wilderness (Lk. 4:1-13). He is constantly involved in the accusations against the "brethren" (Rev. 12:10-12). Scripture contains additional evidence of his ongoing activity. The point is that Satan operates from somewhere, and that somewhere is not Third Heaven. Neither, arguably, is it the first heaven. The logical conclusion is that Satan operates his campaigns of murder and lies from Second Heaven.

We cannot argue outright that Satan rules Second Heaven. We *can* argue, however, that he is currently a resident there. We also see evidence of a kind of war yet to come (Rev. 12:7-9), a war that is waged "in heaven." There is no *a priori* reason to suppose that the Creator of "the heavens and the earth" would permit such a war to occur in Third Heaven. In fact, the opposite would appear to be true.[12] If this is so, then the heavenly war will be waged in Second Heaven, and at its conclusion Satan will be exiled to the earth with his angelic/demonic followers in tow.

Furthermore, the messenger sent from Third Heaven to speak to Daniel (Dan. 10:11-13) encountered hostile resistance on his way to Daniel until Michael came to his aid. It seems likely that this conflict did not occur in Third Heaven; nor is it likely to have occurred in First Heaven. That only leaves Second Heaven, as the passage clearly does not refer to the earth.

45

Second Heaven, then, may be a realm in which Satan currently resides and carries out his wrathful will against mankind. If so, it is highly unlikely that he is unwatched or exercises unfettered liberty to do whatever he wants. It is reasonable to assume, therefore, that other kinds of angels than his own underlings are also in Second Heaven as guarantors of some sort.

First Heaven

In some ways, this is the easiest of the three heavens to discuss. The first heaven (First Heaven) must be the realm spoken of in Genesis 1:15 concerning the great lights. These great lights (sun and moon) and the lesser lights (stars) were made to be visible on the earth. They are, then, *sensible* to us, meaning that we can interact with them with our ordinary physical senses. This heaven, being visible, serves as a place for certain governing signs to aid us in certain areas, such as in understanding how time works. As far as we know, there are no inhabitants of the first heaven. Its primary purpose seems to be to "contain" the earth and provide it with a sensible existence. Forces such as heat, light, gravity, and so forth enable the earth to exist in an orderly, physical manner.

To be clear, the "heavens" in Genesis 1:1 cannot apply only to First Heaven, but must include Second and Third Heaven as well. There is no reason to suppose this realm, First Heaven, the physical universe, would have any native inhabitants who are supernatural in their essential being. Angels, for example, being supernatural beings, are also found to not be native inhabitants of First Heaven, but of Third Heaven. It might be true that some are native to Second Heaven, but that is not clear in scripture. At this point, we might infer from our previous analysis that the angels (Satanic or otherwise) are "trans-plants" to Second Heaven and perhaps only commissioned visitors to First Heaven.

The creation narrative suggests that First Heaven is primarily a place for earth. The fourth day of creation seems to be the time when

First Heaven was put fully into operation. It was to contain the lights that govern how the earth as an entity would operate (Gen. 1:14-19). It is not evident that such a sphere would require the presence of angels of any type.

The Realms of Creation

Third Heaven (the realm where GOD's throne is located)

Second Heaven (the realm where Satan and his angels reside?)

First Heaven (the physical universe as we typically think of it)

Earth (a subset of First Heaven)

There is, however, a supernatural being indigenous to First Heaven. That being is man. As we shall see in a later chapter of this book, the key to the life of man is the breath of GOD in him. His flesh is not the prime component of man's life. To be sure, the physical universe influences the flesh of man and the natural life that is lived by that flesh. However, as I shall argue later in this work, man is spirit first, and spirit is not governed by First Heaven. Spirit is governed only by Third Heaven.

So we have these three heavens: First Heaven (in the physical universe), Second Heaven (a realm that includes wars of a spiritual kind), and Third Heaven (in which GOD has installed a throne from which He rules all The Creation). First Heaven contains everything necessary to maintain the physical integrity of the earth and of the things that live in the earth. Third Heaven contains everything necessary for The Creation to know the GOD of The Creation and experience His sovereign rule. Second Heaven seems to be a realm in which conflict is birthed and sent into the earth where man is. Generally, this conflict pits the soul of man against the spirit of man.

Tripartite Man

The apostle Paul, addressing the new church in Thessaloniki, revealed an important insight when he defined human beings in terms of three "components": spirit, soul, and body (1 Thess. 5:23). While delving into the meanings and distinctions of these three components is beyond the scope of this work, we can say that the three somehow work together to comprise what we call a tripartite nature for man.

In man is the *spirit*, which is derived directly from the breath of GOD that was breathed into Adam at the time of his creation. We'll cover that in a later chapter. In man also is a *body*, which may be usefully thought of as a covering for the spirit. We might conceive of a human being as a spirit wearing a body composed of flesh. Again, this is a topic for another chapter of this work, but this preview may aid us in seeing a useful thing about the heavens.

But what about the *soul* of a man? How may we describe it? One useful direction would be to discuss the soul as the place where the exigencies of the life we live in the flesh body come into "contact" with what we know in our spirit. The body of flesh exists and houses the person in a very physical context. The natural body can, for example, experience a broken arm. The trauma of a broken arm is quite painful and requires immediate attention. In essence the body is screaming (figuratively) that we focus single-mindedly on ameliorating the situation with the arm. For a little while, nothing else is more important. One of the functions of the soul is to bring understanding to the situation and begin to find a remedy for it. The soul helps the person toward resolution of a problem in the body. To a great degree the soul performs this function most of the time. It is the place where physical impacts in life are considered and resolution sought when something is physically wrong. In this sense, the soul is a very useful component of the person. Its eyes are "in the dirt" but it helps us in our physical nature. The soul also, though, gets involved in the not so physical aspects of our lives. After all, it has our best interests at heart, right?

We all experience many feelings in life; a wide range of emotions. These help us interpret the more subtle aspects of physical life.[13] For example, if another person insults you, you experience hurt feelings. Your soul, out of its concern for your well-being, begins to interpret what went on in the event and tries to minimize its impact on you. There are any number of mechanisms it may use, but the point is that the soul "kicks in" to solve this problem just as it did for the broken arm.

Note that in both of these examples all the information came from the physical self. That "self" felt some hurt and the soul moved to find a solution as quickly as possible. Note also that the soul did not seek or receive any spiritual information; it simply acted on the basis of the pain inflicted from the natural environment. Over time, as we experience life, we find that it has certain patterns. Those patterns of things that occur enable us to develop patterns of response as directed by the soul. That's where the trouble lies. The more subtle hurts begin to demand immediate attention even though they are not physically painful.

If left alone, the soul will develop habits for us that totally discount any spiritual input to the situations we encounter in life. We easily become spiritually deaf and blind. In that condition, feelings govern basically all our responses. As a consequence, we become unable to hear any input from our spirit. The spirit functions to keep us in touch with the mind, will, and ways of GOD. It is pleased to guide us in life using the soul as a sort of interpreter. The soul is often unable to hear that information, though, and even justifies ignoring the spirit on the basis that problems need to be solved "right now." When we are spirit-deaf, there is a conflict in our lives. We cannot be influenced by our spirit if we will not or cannot hear our spirit. In the absence of that information, the soul will lead us to care only about our natural lives. Remember that the flesh is only a garment for the true person–the spirit. When the soul will not allow the flesh to hear what the spirit has to say in a matter, it's like the garment telling its wearer what to do. In this is great error.

49

It is important, however, to discuss further the relationship between the spirit and the soul from the perspective of the soul. Our discussion so far has emphasized a soul that seeks to operate independently of the spirit of the man. That is certainly the dominant trend in human beings. We may ask, however, is this the original design of the soul? Another way of looking at this is to ask, does the soul just "happen" (in the same sense as gravity for example)? Is the soul nothing more than the typical outcome of the reasoning capabilities of a human being? Or did GOD very deliberately place the soul in the man for some divine purpose? If the latter be so, then it is important for us to understand that purpose.

An analysis of the first passage in the Bible that speaks of the soul yields some interesting insights. When GOD breathed life into the inert material of the first man's body, the man "became a living being" (Gen. 2:7). The Hebrew word translated "being" in the passage is *nephesh*, which in most English language versions of the Bible is translated as "soul." GOD breathed the divine breath of life into the man and he became a *living soul*. This might be read rather casually, but one of the results of the breath of life being breathed into the dust from which the man was formed was a soul. There is then a linkage between the spirit and the soul that we should examine more closely.

If GOD knew that the result of His breath endowment was to produce something that could be called a "living soul," then we might ask why this result came about and why it matters. Apparently, GOD intended for the soul of the man to come into being when the spirit was breathed into the flesh. Because everything God does is purposeful, it is highly unlikely that the soul was just somehow an unintended or unfortunate side effect of the giving of life. It might be alright to say that the soul was a side effect, but not that it was not in the mind of GOD at the time, because obviously it was. Otherwise, we would be implying that GOD was careless or wicked.

Having established that the soul of man was in the mind of GOD when He breathed life into the man, why might it have been so? As we shall see a bit later, the man was intended to be the representation of

GOD in the earth component of the creation. The man, I will argue, had the nature of GOD built into him in the spirit of the man. The soul then seems to be some sort of link between the one earthly creature who has a spiritual nature and the rest of the creatures in the earth. One obvious conclusion is that the soul was in some manner to be a mechanism through which the spiritual would be seen in the natural. In that view, the soul of man was designed to be a kind of window through which the other creatures in The Creation would see their Creator. This was at least true in the earth, where every other creature was created without a spirit.

In that sense, The Creation was to be enabled to view the very nature of GOD in the life and actions of the man creature. It was GOD's intention that man would perfectly represent GOD within The Creation. Later in this work I will refer to man as the *viceroy* of GOD in this regard. That being so, GOD deliberately gave man a soul so that man's nature would show forth the nature of GOD; to present the "image and likeness" of GOD (Gen. 1:26).

Expanding this view of man requires that we examine the soul in its workings. Initially, the man in the garden of Eden carried out his functions in The Creation according to his "design." GOD told him to have dominion and then he had dominion. Operationally, this began by his naming of the various animals as GOD sent them to him for that purpose. But soon we see the emergence of what we call *reasoning*. When Satan used the serpent to present his arguments to the woman, she *reasoned within her soul*. She knew what the mandate was, but she considered the specific arguments presented to her concerning a specific fruit (Gen. 3:6). She *reasoned* from the physical evidence before her that the fruit was pleasant to look at and that it was probably good to eat. Then she *reasoned*, based on the serpent's arguments, that eating it would make her wise, perhaps as wise as GOD.

It was in this third reasoning that the soul of the woman fell into the trap of her enemy. In the first two reasonings, the stimulus and outcome were simply observations. In the third instance, she wanted a thing that her spirit did not prompt her to have because it was illicit.

It is not reasonable to propose that her flesh wanted this non-physical result. She thought to become other than what GOD had created her to be. When she acted on the basis of that desire, her soul obscured the influence of her spirit. In that moment, her soul acted independently of her spirit. A consequence of that action was that the woman (and, shortly, the man with her) had now failed to present an accurate representation of GOD inside The Creation. Her soul, the middle ground between the flesh and the spirit, if you will, failed of its purpose. This middle ground had complied with the misrepresentations that came out of Second Heaven, and man had fallen, much as Satan had fallen from Third Heaven. Now, from that time onward, man would experience inner conflict because his soul was often at war with his spirit. The *spirit* knows the will of GOD. The *soul* often spurns the will of GOD. The *flesh* eats and sleeps and such.

Man and the Heavens

Consider the following proposition: the three heavens are each parallel to one of the three "parts" of the human being. We can visualize it this way:

Human *spirit* is parallel to Third Heaven, characterized by the rule of GOD.

Human *soul* is parallel to Second Heaven, characterized by spiritual conflict.

Human *flesh* (body) is parallel to First Heaven, characterized by death and corruption.

Third Heaven is characterized by the absolute will and nature of GOD. In it is found that which is absolutely best for the human being. That is manifested in the human spirit. Second Heaven is non-corporeal in nature, as is Third Heaven. However, Second Heaven contains within it a primary source of conflict. It is now "home" to the father of

52

lies, Satan. For that reason spiritual conflicts are generated there. The bulk of the conflicts in our lives are found in the soul, not in the body or the spirit. Second Heaven will be rid of conflict when Satan is exiled from it (Rev. 12:12). In the meantime, conflict between the will of GOD and its execution in the earth will remain. Even so, conflict will remain in the human soul until the absolute triumph of the spirit. It is the nature of our human existence to be deceived into making poor decisions that produce spiritual turmoil for us. The only way out of this is to learn to make the will of GOD in our lives, as revealed from Third Heaven, immune to the conflicts of the soul that are sourced in Second Heaven. In this, His will is done "in earth as it is in heaven."

The body wants what the body wants. When we are thirsty, we want to quench our thirst. Generally we will not perceive that in any spiritual light. As the apostle Paul asked, "*Who will set me free from the body of this death?*" (Rom. 7:24) As we shall see later, the body is inanimate matter borrowed for but a while until it returns to its natural inanimate state. The undisciplined soul, though, will respond to the exigencies of the body preferentially over the wisdom of the spirit until the soul is retrained. The body is parallel to First Heaven in its absolute inability to be free of its death nature.

When GOD breathed the life of His Spirit into the dirt of which the first man was physically composed, He caused the man to parallel The Creation itself in its various realms. Our Father is a Master Planner. He pointed at the whole creation in the person of a human being.

Angels

The biblical text leaves us with no doubt that GOD created angels to inhabit The Creation. Some may argue that angels existed prior to the coming into being of The Creation. This would place angels in the context we have called The Eternity. We cannot, with all certainty, rule out that angels of some sort have been in The Eternity with GOD. That seems to be unnecessary, however. It is difficult to imagine what purpose angels would perform in that context.

If angels preceded the acts of creation, then they were always present with GOD. We dare not posit fallibility or finitude as properties to be found in The Eternal. If that be so, then angels who preceded The Creation would be essentially equivalent to GOD Himself. This does not seem like a reasonable proposition.

Another condition required by the idea of pre-existing angels is that some of them must have been called into service once The Creation got under way. In this model, angels would be with GOD in The Eternity. Then, when He set out to bring The Creation into being, at least some of those angels would be "sent" into the new context, The Creation, to be whatever they were to be in that context. In this model, some angels might remain in The Eternity or all might be sent into The Creation. Again, this is a bit unsettling even if it turns out to be the case.

The more likely situation is that angels were created within the acts of creation and are co-incident with The Creation. If this is true, then all the angels are found to be located somewhere "inside" The Creation. Following this line of reasoning, The Creation gives purpose to the creation of angels. Their existence is not independent of The Creation. From this perspective, there were no angels before the acts of creation began. Furthermore, The Creation would not be complete without the presence of angels in it. From these facts we can deduce some conclusions concerning angels.

Characteristics of Angels

One of the apparent conclusions regarding angels is that they are localized phenomena. This means that they are in some particular place at some particular time. They may move from place to place with rapidity that we cannot comprehend. They may move without our comprehension or detection of their movement. In limited cases, and for particular purposes, we may, however, detect their movement. For example, when Abraham was visited by three visitors (Gen. 18), he perceived (saw) that two of them walked away from him toward Sodom.

Shortly after that time, Lot also witnessed the progress of the same two angels (Gen. 19) until he was well on his way away from Sodom. This is an important property of angels in terms of their interactions with mankind. They can be perceived, even sometimes being thought to be men, as in the Abraham story just cited. Sometimes humans converse with angels, as Mary clearly did (Lk. 1:26-38). In fact, the very word "angel" may sometimes indicate a human being, as the word itself simply means "messenger."

Some may object that angels are spiritual beings and therefore *localized* only in dealing with human beings. This seems unlikely when we consider the scene in Revelation 4 and 5. Even more cogently, Daniel was visited by an angel who testified to the difficulty of his journey through the heavens to come to Daniel (Dan. 10:1-12). By the way, this angel looked like a man to Daniel.

Another characteristic of angels is that they can move about anywhere within The Creation in performance of their functions. They are apparently not bound to any one realm within The Creation. For example, the angels Jacob saw (Gen. 28:12) as he was departing Canaan to go to his uncle in Paddan-aram, were moving back and forth between the realms of earth and Third Heaven. The Daniel passage just mentioned also involved angels moving between and among the various realms, of which earth is only one. This capability is not necessarily unlimited and it might be they can transcend the bounds of realms only in pursuit of their responsibilities. In any event, however, their duties seem often to require just such a capability.

Angels are not what we call "mortal." Mortality seems to be a property of the realm of earth. Its living inhabitants die a physical death. That death returns the stuff of their bodies to its original status. One of the results of mortality is that continuity demands reproduction. In the case of man, reproduction is a very positive thing as it is the mechanism through which the phenomenon of fathers and sons is lived out in the earth as a picture of the relationship between GOD the Father and GOD the Son in the Godhead. In fact, JESUS emphasized exactly that relationship in His work among the Jewish people.

This matters to us because the angels stand in contrast to mankind. JESUS revealed that angels neither reproduce (see Mt. 22:30 and Lk. 20:34-36) nor die. If angels do not die (they are not wrapped in flesh), it seems reasonable to expect that they will exist individually until such time as the realm into which they were placed at the time of their creation ceases to exist in its current form. To clarify, whatever was created as a part of The Creation is subject to the will of the Creator. Scripture strongly indicates that the entire creation eventually will be returned to The Eternal through some kind of transformation that we do not understand.[14] When that event takes place, it is quite possible that angels will not be as they are now even if they maintain some sort of individual existence.

While we do not know what the transformations to come will be like, Peter assures us that there will be new heavens and a new earth (2 Pet. 3:7-13).[15] Whether the new heavens and new earth will be eternal in and of themselves is not clear from scripture. For our purposes, we should note that angels apparently will continue for as long as The Creation remains, even after it is transformed into its "new" state.

We generally think of angels as messengers. Indeed, in most of the cases of their appearances in scripture, they are carrying information from the heavens to humans in the earth. This, of course, is not their only function. For example, angels tended to JESUS at the end of the temptation cycle (Mt. 4:11). The ministrations of the angels in this situation are not described, but it seems clear that normal "messengering" was not the agenda. JESUS already knew the mind of GOD.

In any event the affairs and welfare of human beings are a consideration in the labors of the angels. The writer of Hebrews even claims that all angels are spiritual beings sent to serve the inheritors of salvation (Heb. 1:14). This implies that the "messenger" function is a subset of the general category of ministering. So angels minister to those humans who are inheriting salvation.

Angels also stand in the presence of GOD in the throne room in Third Heaven (Rev. 5:11). They have also been known to appear before GOD in some sort of accountability meetings (Job 1:6; 2:6). It is not reasonable to assume angels can appear outside The Creation. They must, then, have appeared in Third Heaven to give account before GOD in the Job narrative.

The "native habitat" of angels seems to be Third Heaven. They definitely appear not to be native to First Heaven, but often are sent to First Heaven from somewhere else. Angels appear in very large numbers in Third Heaven in John's vision recorded in Revelation (Rev. 5:11). They also do not seem to be native to Second Heaven, but I will argue that it is the current abode of Satan and those angels who *fell* with him from Third Heaven. Even for those angels, however, Third Heaven seems to have been their original location. As I mentioned before, Jacob in his dream saw angels ascending to Third Heaven from the earth (Gen. 28:12). The other end of the ladder must have been in Third Heaven because Jacob saw GOD at the top of the ladder. For lack of scriptural evidence to the contrary, let us assume that the native habitat of angels is Third Heaven and that those who did not fall with Satan are still headquartered there. In fact, the verb "fell" that JESUS used to describe Satan's first displacement suggests traversing from the higher or greater (Third) to the lower or lesser (Second) heaven.

When Were the Angels Created?

We cannot answer this question with precision. Surely, they were created within the timeframe of the acts of creation. After GOD finished His work on the sixth day, everything had been created, including angels. I propose that they were created before man.[16] Because scripture is concerned primarily with GOD and man, it does not provide that information specifically.

One way to look at the matter is to assume that the angels were created on the first day along with the unspecified "heavens." After all, the six days of creation are about man, not angels. It is not hard to imagine they were in place by the time man came into view in the earth. In this view, angels came into being only slightly before man. They were not hanging around in eternity just biding their time. They were not needed until the time came for the creation of man.

Satan

One of the angels is an entity called Satan, the devil, and so forth, who figures quite prominently in the saga of mankind. He most likely was created at the same time as all the other angels, probably on the first day of the creative acts. Along with all the other angels, he witnessed the rest of the creative acts as GOD went about the business of preparing the first home for his intended sons. There he was in Third Heaven, witnessing the great work of GOD. It is not likely that he or any of the other angels had much to do except to witness the loving work of GOD in bringing The Creation into full form for the sake of His beloved.

Perhaps when Satan witnessed the breath of life entering the man form, he realized that this newest creature was to be preferred by GOD over the angels, who, while eternal, did not have the divine breath. Perhaps in that moment he came to detest the new creature. We cannot know this one way or the other. It seems plain from the biblical narrative, however, Satan never ministered to man in any positive sense. Every interaction of his with mankind has been negative from the beginning.

The first recorded interaction between Satan and humans was the event involving the fruit of the **tree of the knowledge of good and evil** after man was installed in the garden and the woman was brought forth. There seem to be three possibilities with respect to what was happening with him in the garden narrative. In one scenario, as soon as Satan formed the hate of man in his heart, he was no longer able to stay in Third Heaven and fell to Second Heaven, not necessarily by the direction of GOD but by an incompatibility with the substance of Third Heaven. One may almost perceive it as a type of gravitational force that pulled him out of Third Heaven "down" to Second Heaven. Another scenario suggests he fell as soon as the temptation occurred. The same "gravitational" effect would explain that fall as well. In yet another scenario, GOD sent him from Third Heaven to Second Heaven as a component of the Eden judgments (Gen. 3:13-19). This last scenario seems unlikely because GOD did not address the serpent with a question. He did not address the serpent in terms of the presence of Satan in what the serpent had done. Furthermore, the serpent was prompted by Satan before the man and woman were actually deceived. His curse, moreover, was not about a fall but about abjection.

Of the three possibilities presented, the most likely one to me is that Satan fell as soon as he began to hate mankind. From his place in Second Heaven, he would carry out his first plot against mankind by prompting the serpent to deceive the woman, perhaps even "inhabiting" the serpent.

Summary

As I mentioned at its beginning, this chapter is an insertion that deals with matters that are primarily tangential to the text of the first eleven chapters of Genesis. However, there are topics that matter to the narrative that have to do with what was going on in the rest of The Creation outside of earth itself. Furthermore, many of these matters are the subjects of questions commonly asked by folks who believe in the biblical narrative and just want to know more about these entities that were so influential even from the very earliest days.

To some extent, the topics covered in this chapter might be thought to "jump the gun" on the narrative. Hopefully, the material in this chapter will broaden your appreciation of some of the topics we will analyze later. You can look back on this material as providing part of the backdrop for events that are to occur later in the creation cycle and in the sometimes awkward saga of the emerging of man in his roles in the earth down to the end times.

---

[1] The earth, in fact, "sits" inside the first level of the heavens. In Jacob's vision in Genesis 28:12 angels appear to move back and forth between heaven and earth. Numerous other passages also speak of angels interacting with man in the earth. Paul and John both "went" to the heavens in some sense.

[2] In Isaiah 66:1-2 GOD informed Isaiah of the futility of building a house for Him anywhere in The Creation. Rather (by implication) He looks to dwell in the hearts of those who have turned humbly towards Him.

[3] According to Revelation 4:1-2, the throne was the first thing John saw and was the center for the things seen in the revelations that followed. This reminds us of Isaiah 66:1 in which GOD announced that the heavens were His throne, not His house.

[4] Matthew 6:9-13 records what we often call "the Lord's Prayer." It is the "model" prayer He gave to His disciples in response to their request. Verse 10 states that GOD's (the Father's) will prevails perfectly and completely in the heavens. In this present study, I claim that this refers to Third Heaven, where the throne of GOD's rule is the centerpiece.

[5] A realm is a defined entity or context, separate and separately identified from other realms in some manner. I argue for four realms in The Creation: three heavens with each heaven a realm in its own right, as well as the earth. This does not preclude the possibility that there might be other realms in The Creation. However, scripture has not directly revealed that to be the case. I propose later in this book that Satan, along with all the other angels, was created in a realm called Third Heaven. After Satan discovered that GOD would love man and prefer man to any angel, he decided to hate man. In so doing, he simply fell from the context of Third Heaven to a context called Second Heaven, where he currently resides. It is as though he became unable to remain in his first home, not that he was sent from it. A suitable metaphor might be that he became too "heavy" to remain and fell to another place.

[6] Revelation 12:9 is not about falling, but about being forcefully expelled.

[7] The last three chapters of Daniel seem to provide a continuous narrative of one sent from the Third Heaven (Dan. 10:12-13) and who forbad the recording of some of the vision (Dan. 12:4).

[8] Each of the heavens and the earth is a realm in its own right, where the rule or mode of rule is different from another realm. In the present case we specify that Third Heaven is a realm apart from Second Heaven and others.

[9] Job 1 and 2 use the term "sons of GOD" in a way not otherwise used. In the Job passages, it seems clear the entities referred to are inhabitants of Third Heaven, not men or some other offspring of GOD. They are "heavenly" beings, and the context may imply that this took place at the throne, which I argue is in the Third Heaven. By contrast, Genesis 6 uses the term "sons of GOD" to refer to the descendants of Seth to distinguish them from the descendants of Cain (see chapter eight).

[10] You and I cannot go to Third Heaven unless there is some special provision made by GOD, as was the case with John in Revelation and with Satan in the Job accounts.

[11] Consider the amazing physical dependence of the earth on the physical universe in such matters as heat and light. It may be argued that what we call the universe is designed exactly to be the "container," if you will, of the earth. From that viewpoint, the universe seemingly has no other purpose.

[12] Revelation 4-5 suggest there is no disagreement with GOD near the throne. Rather, all is harmony and praise there, hardly the context in which wars would be fought. War will be taken to Satan and his followers. They do not have the power to invade Third Heaven, where the will of GOD is absolute.

[13] This is a fairly imprecise summary of these softer matters, but it gets at the general aspects. Whole fields of human endeavor such as psychology have been developed to study such things. We won't deal with psychology and such directly as that is outside the scope of our analysis.

[14] Second Peter 3:10 implies a complete transformation of all of The Creation. This seems compatible with the idea that at the end of things *"God will be all in all"* (1 Cor. 15:28).

[15] Translators use "new heavens" here in spite of the fact that the Greek word is singular, per our discussion of Hebrew and Greek difference.

[16] Certainly no later, as they are ministers to mankind. The Creation seems to have been created as the context for mankind as sons of GOD. All was prepared and brought to maturity before the man was created. Certainly, angels would be in place as well.

CHAPTER THREE

THE WORK CONTINUES (GENESIS 1:6-25)

Light, water, and the *stuff* of everything else, including living beings, were ready when Second Day began. The components were all in place. As the period of light ended on Day One, the Creator moved into the second phase of His acts of creation.

You will recall that during Day One, GOD separated light from darkness as a major testimony to the work of that day. As Second Day began, He furthered the work of separation by commanding that there be a sky to separate the earth from the heavens. On Day One He had created the heavens and the earth, but a clear distinction between the two was still wanting at the end of that day. He commanded that there be an "expanse" to provide that distinction, and the narrative tells us that He *made* the expanse Himself. After He did that, there then existed the earth (still primarily characterized by water), the "expanse," and the heavens, arranged apparently in some sort of concentric configuration.

Second Day (Monday, Abib 2)

Then God said, "Let there be an expanse in the midst of the waters, and let it separate the waters from the waters." God made the expanse, and separated the waters which were below the expanse from the waters which were above the expanse; and it was so. God called the expanse heaven. And there was evening and there was morning, a second day (Genesis 1:6-8).

The creation narrative informs us of the creation of the heavens and the earth on Day One. It specifies that both were created but gives us no information as to how one could be distinguished from the other. Obviously, they provided a matrix onto which the rest of the works of creation were to be constructed by "invention or manufacturing." One interesting feature of the Day One narrative was the specification that "waters" occupied the attention of the Spirit of GOD. But what the "waters" were goes unspecified. GOD also spoke light into being on Day One.

It was to the "waters" that GOD turned His attention on Second Day. One gets the impression that both the earth and the heavens were composed of "waters" and that GOD thought it important to separate the two sets or kinds of "waters." Earth "waters" and heavens "waters" were apparently not the same thing but were in such close proximity that some sort of separation was needed between them.[1]

So what might the "waters" have been? Ordinarily, the word water is not ambiguous although it may be used in a variety of ways. Our notion of water is fairly fixed, and when we use the word in other than the ordinary way, we feel compelled to clarify what we mean. However, in the creation narrative, the word is applied to both the heavens and the earth in such a way as to imply they needed more clarification. In fact, the idea of "waters of the heavens" would be quite difficult to deal with given the way we think about the heavens, or just heaven.

We encounter water on the earth regularly, in the oceans, lakes, rivers, and streams. There is little ambiguity about that. But the "waters" of the heavens needs some explanation. Unfortunately, we cannot fully satisfy whatever curiosity we might have about that. We know enough about space beyond the earth's atmosphere that the idea of its being characterized by anything that corresponds to a watery ocean is puzzling to us.

Let's propose that literal water as we know it on earth can be compared to some significant aspect of space ("the heavens"). In what sense can that be done? One of the interesting properties of liquids, especially of water, is that they have no particular shape in the liquid form (phase is what scientists call it). In its liquid form, water will only take the shape of something that contains it. Without a container, water will continue to spread over wider and wider areas until the volume of water is exhausted. This inherent shapelessness is a fairly important property that water has and makes it particularly useful, for example, in helping to maintain life as we know it. We wouldn't want to drink water if it had sharp edges or was too large to swallow (think large ice cube). In such cases we would want to change it back into the shapeless (formless) liquid.

Space is similar to water in that it is inherently shapeless or formless. It may be given form when we think of it in terms of something that contains it, but without a container of some sort, space will have no shape. Let's propose for the moment that this inherent shapelessness is the property that space has in common with water as we know it. If we go further and propose that the word "waters" is used in Genesis 1 to compare the two of them *based on this property*, the idea of separating them can take on significant meaning. In fact, it appears that if the atmosphere of the earth were suddenly removed, all water would either freeze into the solid form of ice or would immediately be lost to space by rapid evaporation. It would not continue to lie about in liquid form, such as in seas or oceans.

It might be that GOD, who was creating these things, knew quite well that the liquid water of the earth and empty space were simply not compatible in proximity to one another. The absence of some barrier between them would cause inherently shapeless water to seek to take the shape of shapeless space and be totally lost to us. That condition, of course, would eliminate life as we know it. Because GOD knew that "life" was a key component of His goal, this would not be a workable situation. So He had to prevent it during the works of creation. The solution He chose was to place something between the water on earth and the "waters" (shapeless condition) of space. That something would protect the water from disappearing. It is beyond our current scope to do so, but this discussion of water (and space) provides significant metaphorical material for consideration of all manner of spiritual phenomena.

In this scenario, the ingenious solution of GOD was to place a lid on the liquid water of earth to prevent its escape into space. In this way shapeless water would be protected from shapeless space. This lid, though, needed to permit the other things GOD would do on the earth in the upcoming days (3 through 6) of creation and thereafter. For one thing, it needed to permit life. The water lid (separator) GOD decided on was what we call the atmosphere. It is dense enough at the surface of earth waters that it keeps them from flying off into space. At the same time, it is quite permeable to the presence of other objects. In fact, it shares the property of shapelessness with water and space, which it was made to separate. The creation narrative uses the word "expanse" to express this phenomenon. Most folks would agree that expanse and atmosphere can be used interchangeably here. This interpretation, we should keep in mind, is necessarily limited as nearly as possible to the literal meaning of the text. Again, metaphors of many kinds may come to mind.

An interesting phrase appears in Genesis 1:2: the "surface of the deep." On the face of it, the word "deep" would seem to refer to things like seas or oceans. But the rest of that verse speaks of the "surface of the waters." Are the two phrases redundant? If so, why is the Spirit of GOD only spoken of in the context of the second term? What if "deep" is actually a term referring to something other than water? What if "deep" refers to an apparently endless unknown of what we now call space?[2] In that case, the surface of the deep would refer to a beginning of space, the point beyond which space would "begin." As we have seen, this makes good sense when we examine the nature of the atmosphere.

Let's pull things together again. On Day One GOD created both the heavens and the earth. The fact that the "Spirit of God was moving over the surface of the waters" (Gen. 1:2) may well imply (among other things) that the entire surface of what we know as the earth was covered with water. He (the Spirit of GOD) might have been a sort of guardian between the "surface of the deep" and the "surface of the waters" until the atmosphere was completed on Second Day. In the two terms, the word "surface" may refer to the boundary between the two. In this paradigm, Day One saw the creation of water, space, some undifferentiated solid material, and light. Second Day saw the insertion of an expanse we now call the atmosphere at the boundary between the two "surfaces." GOD began to impose more order on the basic materials of creation.

What we have called "atmosphere" contained materials that gave it the weight to be a "lid" for the waters that covered the surface of the earth. Those materials are the various gases of which air is composed. They include, primarily, nitrogen, oxygen, and carbon dioxide. Interestingly, all these materials are vital to life as we know it.

What we call the sky is an optical effect that occurs as we look through the atmosphere. The expanse can be thought of as an atmosphere composed of air which appears to have a boundary that we call the sky. That sky boundary occurs where the atmosphere ends and space begins, for all practical purposes. The surfaces are not smooth but they do work.

For us:

Expanse = atmosphere

Atmosphere includes air and "sky"

As was the case on Day One, Second Day began with a dark period that we would now call night. That (Sunday) night ended with the coming of the light period of Monday morning. This work of creating the atmosphere to separate a water-covered earth from space took place during that period of "evening and morning." While its accuracy is not fully verifiable, the paradigm presented in this and the previous chapters is consistent with what we have in the Genesis 1 creation narrative itself.

At the end of Second Day (Monday sundown), several crucial works had been finished. On these would be built progressively the rest of The Creation. All of these works were good things, but GOD singled out light especially to call "good."

Third Day (Tuesday, Abib 3)

> *Then God said, "Let the waters below the heavens be gathered into one place, and let the dry land appear"; and it was so. God called the dry land earth, and the gathering of the waters He called seas; and God saw that it was good. Then God said, "Let the earth sprout vegetation: plants yielding seed, and fruit trees on the earth bearing fruit after their kind with seed in them"; and it was so. The earth brought forth vegetation, plants yielding seed after their kind, and trees bearing fruit with seed in them, after their kind; and God saw that it was good. There was evening and there was morning, a third day (Genesis 1:9-13).*

On the third day of creation acts, GOD brought about two major outcomes: introduction of land and introduction of the first living things.

Phase One:

On the first part of Third Day, GOD said, and it came about. GOD then saw the good in it. By the end of Second Day (equivalent to sundown on a Monday), GOD had brought forth things that were necessary to the sustenance of life: water, air, and light. Third Day was given over to the production of solid surfaces (land) and the earliest life forms. Some of those life forms could live in the water, but some needed land in order to live and perform their functions. Before land-based plant life could be brought into being, it was necessary that there be land. So, land was the first work of Third Day (basically a Tuesday to us).

The first chapter of Genesis suggests that the earth was entirely covered with water at the time of creation (Gen. 1:2) when it presents the Spirit of GOD as hovering over the surface of the waters. The "waters" in this case covered what was later to be land mass and all the other solid materials of the newly-created earth. The suggestion of some persons that the earth was not covered by water argues against the clear sense of Genesis 1:9, which strongly implies that the gathering process on Third Day somehow caused some land areas to rise above the waters. By implication, this would cause watery areas to become deeper to hold the now displaced water.

Almost certainly, the raising up of solid earth material was the result of earth shifting. The obvious causes would be earthquakes or volcanoes. When such geological (tectonic) activities occur, they often result in shifts in the relative positions of solid masses. Such shifts often result in some areas rising and some areas descending. In our situation, the rising land masses came up out of the covering waters while the descending land masses permitted displaced water to move into them. The result was that land areas and water areas were present simultaneously; the seas were distinguished from dry land. While water is inherently shapeless, land is not. Now the land could begin to partially "define" the water by delimiting it.

It is intriguing to think that maybe there was but one land mass at this original separation between sea and dry land. Eden needed only one continent upon which to exist. The creation of man, to occur several days later, would occur in only one place. Even science seems to suggest that a single land mass occurred first and was later broken up due to tectonic forces. These forces were such, they say, that the subsequent masses (continents perhaps) were forced great distances apart. In a later chapter of this book we will consider what went on during the great flood. Again, scientific theory is quite compatible with the mechanics and outcomes, just not the duration of the events.

The separation between land and water was good in the sight of GOD. This is the second time scripture attaches the specific adjective "good" to the work of GOD. Light was good and the land/sea separation was good in His eyes. The "good" works of GOD are listed below. Note that all the works of creation were good in the eyes of GOD insofar as the creation narrative is concerned. However, these were specified as such:

The Works Called "Good"			
<u>Work</u>	<u>Status</u>	<u>Day</u>	<u>Verse</u>
Light spoken into being	Good	One	3
Land raised out of water	Good	Three	10
Reproductive plant life	Good	Three	12
Luminaries to conquer darkness	Good	Four	18
Air and water animals	Good	Five	21
Land animals	Good	Six	25
Man	Very Good	Six	31

These separations between light and dark, earth and the heavens, and evening and morning were all part of the matrix of phenomena that supported the arrival of living beings. Interestingly, the sequence of events is similar to those proposed by scientific theory, just not the duration of time involved. GOD had set the stage for life. According to the creation narrative, it had taken about two and one-half days.

Phase Two:

On the second part of Third Day, GOD said, and it came about. He then saw the good in it. Land, water, light, and air; what else was needed? Now GOD had the conditions that made life possible. The first form of life was plant life. Although the creation narrative does not say so, it is likely that the plant life that came forth included both waterborne (e.g. algae) and land-borne (e.g. trees). The emphasis, of course, is on the typical land-based food fare for the animals that were soon to be created; especially grain and fruit-bearing trees. We must assume they were mature before the "eaters" were created. If these are literal days, then plant life was brought forth in a mature format.

Fourth Day (Wednesday, Abib 4)

> *Then God said, "Let there be lights in the expanse of the heavens to separate the day from the night, and let them be for signs and for seasons and for days and years; and let them be for lights in the expanse of the heavens to give light on the earth"; and it was so. God made the two great lights, the greater light to govern the day, and the lesser light to govern the night; He made the stars also. God placed them in the expanse of the heavens to give light on the earth, and to govern the day and the night, and to separate the light from the darkness; and God saw that it was good. There was evening and there was morning, a fourth day (Genesis 1:14-19).*

On Fourth Day GOD said what He wanted and He made it. He then saw that it was good.

Fourth Day was set aside for the introduction (making) of what we might call heavenly luminaries: sun, moon, and stars (this probably includes what we call comets). It was the determination of GOD that these luminary bodies were to provide light, but He also determined other functions for them.

1. To separate day from night
2. To be signs
3. To participate in governing seasons
4. To define days
5. To define years

On Day One GOD spoke light into being. He separated light from darkness Himself. Furthermore, He called the light period day and the dark period night (verse 5), thus making a distinction between light and dark with the naming of the two main periods of the day.

That was on Sunday. Fourth Day began at sundown on Tuesday and extended through the sundown of Wednesday. On Fourth Day that work continued. He set about the business of making the heavenly sources of natural light.

Again, let's remember that light simply existed inside The Creation after Day One. It had no specified source; it simply *was* by GOD's command. Now, on Wednesday (Fourth Day), GOD created the source of light that determined the light period of the day and the source that determined the dark period of the day. The dark period also had light, but less than did the light period. (Obviously, the word "day" has two meanings in the narrative and in this discussion. It means *both* the entire 24-hour period of a day and the shorter light period of the day. We should be comfortable with this, but let's keep in mind that both meanings pertain here. Evening and morning are more definite in their meanings, but night and day are the terms used here.) Let's be clear. On Day One GOD caused day and night via the introduction of light, but the light had no identified natural source. On Fourth Day, the work was the *making of the sources* for each kind of natural light. He spoke light into being, and He made its sources three days later. Even in darkness there was now to be some light ordinarily. On Day One the distinction between light and darkness was stark and we may infer there was no light in the dark periods. After Fourth Day, this was no longer be the case. The light sources would always provide light so that darkness could never fully prevail again. At a spiritual level, this parallels John's statement of the triumph of Light over darkness (Jn. 1:5). Let's remember that we discovered earlier there is no darkness in The Eternal, nor will any be necessary in the New Jerusalem (Rev. 22:23), which will proceed to the earth from the heavens.

GOD even created lesser lights (stars) to accompany the two greater lights (sun and moon). The sun and moon would "rule" day and night. The lesser lights basically supplement the moon, at least for non-city dwellers. Darkness would no longer prevail at any time of day. Light would always penetrate the darkness. Interestingly, darkness does not penetrate light. Darkness can only prevail when there is no light present. Light always wins.

The luminary bodies (luminaries) exist in the heavens by the way. They are not in or from the earth. GOD placed them in the context of the heavens (First Heaven) for the benefit of the earth, thus pointing to a divine principle that The Creation is designed to serve the sons of GOD. From our perspective, when we see the luminaries, they seem to be very near, as though they were in the atmosphere. This has to do with the fact that we are actually seeing the impact of the light from the luminaries as that light interacts with our atmosphere. From our perspective, they seem to be where the atmosphere meets outer space. However, they exist in what we are calling First Heaven.

So the luminaries are sources (centers) of light. They are never dark. The most potent "lightness" is at their surfaces. As long as they exist, from the moment GOD made them, they will be those places from which natural light goes forth. In a sense (and only for purposes of clearer understanding) it is as though GOD had taken the light He had created on Day One and concentrated it into certain points for perpetual emittance. In so doing, He made possible the various functions of the luminaries listed above. Light is not what does these things. The luminary bodies (*sources* of light) are the entities designed to perform the functions specified in the narrative.

We humans have never experienced the world with un-sourced light. We have known light only in terms of its sources (e.g. sunlight, moonlight). The obvious relationship of heavenly-sourced light to functions 1 and 4 above is almost instinctual for us. In fact, we most often think of light in terms of "daylight and dark" as the presence or absence of the sun in the sky at any particular moment.

Fifth Day (Thursday, Abib 5)

Then God said, "Let the waters teem with swarms of living creatures, and let birds fly above the earth in the open expanse of the heavens." God created the great sea monsters and every living creature that moves, with which the waters swarmed after their kind, and every winged

> *bird after its kind; and God saw that it was good. God*
> *blessed them, saying, "Be fruitful and multiply, and fill*
> *the waters in the seas, and let birds multiply on the earth."*
> *There was evening and there was morning, a fifth day*
> *(Genesis 1:20-23).*

The primary work of Fifth Day (Wednesday evening and Thursday) was the bringing into being (by speaking) of waterborne and airborne life forms. The swimming things and the flying things came into being on that day. (At least most of them did.) It is not clear to us how GOD accomplished these feats, in the sense that He spoke and then He created them. There is a strong implication in the text that GOD envisioned and made a very large diversity that included the smallest crustaceans and mollusks up to the largest swimming things in the water. The requirements for airborne organisms make them much less numerous in kind, but the text still implies a full panoply of creatures.

Properly, in the text, the airborne population is specified by the single word "bird." The implication, though, is that things like flying insects and flying mammals were included under the same heading. This might be a bit of a challenge to strict taxonomists, but it seems to suit the meaning. My contention is that this is the meaning being conveyed.

The nouns related to waterborne life are more inclusive, with language like "swarms of living creatures" and "great sea creatures" (Gen. 1:20-21). The latter is likely to include such animals as whales, for example. The point is that the reference is not to fish alone, but to whatever animals live their lives primarily in the water, either salt or fresh. This would include unknown creatures referred to as "sea monsters" (leviathan) in the text (Gen. 1:21). Much speculation has gone into what these things are. This is not the context in which to try to solve that riddle. By the way, all the water was fresh at the beginning because the processes that add salt to seawater were not yet under way.

What I have said is that this passage (Gen. 1:20-22) uses broad language to indicate quite an array of new creatures. It is impractical in such passages to refer to all the kinds of waterborne creatures, for example. The point is to convey that on Fifth Day GOD populated the seas, rivers, and lakes with every form of life that lives in the water. Water in general, and in every specific kind, contains a vast myriad of life forms that perform a dizzying array of functions, many of which are very important to life. GOD simply saw to it that they came to be. So there were "swarms of living creatures" that He brought into being.

What happens in the air is not as complex biologically as what happens in water. Life as we know it needs air, but the maintenance of air is simply not as dependent on biological action as is the maintenance of water. This is not meant to trivialize such things as oxygen and carbon dioxide balances, which do depend on biological factors, but the complexity overall is just not there.

Sixth Day (Friday, Abib 6)

> *Then God said, "Let the earth bring forth living creatures after their kind: cattle and creeping things and beasts of the earth after their kind"; and it was so. God made the beasts of the earth after their kind, and the cattle after their kind, and everything that creeps on the ground after its kind; and God saw that it was good (Genesis 1:24-25).*

This chapter will end with the first phase of Sixth Day. The creation of man will be the subject of the next chapter. Sixth Day consisted of what we call Thursday evening and Friday until evening. On Sixth Day, GOD spoke and then He made.

Phase One:

GOD spoke and then made the land-based animals as His last acts before creating man. The obvious relationship between man and land-based animals seems clearly to support their immediate temporal juxtaposition in the creation narrative. The text strongly implies that GOD created animals of all sizes in the first part of the day. At the risk of being too pedantic, it might be that flying insects were created on Fifth Day and insects that only crawl were created on Sixth Day. That is a minor taxonomic consideration, but a consideration nonetheless. In this sense, bats would be Fifth Day creatures and rodents would be Sixth Day creatures. The very broad language used to portray such massive works leaves us with some ambiguity in this matter.

The previous considerations leave us with the question of whether GOD followed strict taxonomic distinctions or whether He was more concerned with environmental considerations. It is not likely that we can know such things, but they are more academic than practical in nature anyway. So in the earlier parts of Sixth Day GOD created insects, reptiles, amphibians, and mammals, generally. Specific exceptions to this statement are simply not clear to us. The precise specification of all Fifth Day and Sixth Day *manufacturing* leaves us wondering. Would flightless birds wait until Sixth Day, for example? Were the flying insects made on Fifth Day or were they held for Sixth Day along with crawling insects? While it would be of some interest to know such things with precision, they are not the core of the creation narrative, and we will leave them unknown.

When considering the narrative of creation, people always ask about the dinosaurs. Ample physical evidence exists to require some sort of inclusion of these creatures in the creation narrative. Fossil finds also abound for a wide range of plant life that no longer exists.[3] Concern over the dinosaurs exists though because of the flood narrative found in Genesis chapters 6-8. This distinct narrative specifies the preservation of animal life through the actions of Noah and his sons. Because the category "dinosaur" no longer exists as living organisms on the earth, we assume their extinction before or during the flood. If they were preserved on the ark, the reasoning goes, why would they no longer be present on the earth today? To the extent we can, we will analyze that issue later in this book. For now, let's suggest that the general category "dinosaur" was created in the early part of Sixth Day, along with the rest of the land-based life forms. They may, however, have come forth only after the expulsion of Cain from Eden, as we shall see.

Let's move on now to the section of the creation narrative that pertains to man. This is the created being which GOD put into place to be eligible to become "sons of GOD." Rightfully then, the creation of man is the last part of the narrative. After this ultimate act of creation, GOD would be finished. The basic statements regarding the creation of man are contained in Genesis 1:26-31. Immediately following that passage, an expanded view of it is to be found in the second chapter of Genesis. These will be the matters of the next chapter of this book.

---

[1] From a physical perspective, this is not a distinction we can entirely understand. One line of investigation suggests that "waters" refers to some entity that was fluid and unshaped in and of itself. Water as we think of it only has shape when it is placed into a container. In fact, the container imposes its shape on the water. Outer space appears to have the same characteristic. In and of itself, it has no shape. Rather, it "fills" whatever is not filled by something else. Where water exists, it fills whatever space is not occupied by something else until its volume is exhausted. Outer space is coincident with what we call vacuum. If water is exposed to a vacuum, it will become disassociated molecules rather than a fluid. Thus, in the absence of a separation, water would leave the earth and become fully disassociated in outer space. This might be a physical explanation of the meaning of Genesis 1:6. In this case, spiritual meanings would differ from physical ones.

[2] There are theological implications as well. GOD may be thought of as the "deep" in the context of His apparently indefinable state. That would somehow liken Him to apparently boundless and indefinable space. Space is probably not unbounded, as some suppose, but we have no way to find its bounds as physical beings, nor is it necessary that we do so.

[3] When Cain was exiled from Eden (see chapter 7), he went into a context that was cursed because of Adam, and he himself was cursed from the land. At this point, I present a simple hypothesis. I propose that the rules that worked in Eden did not work outside Eden. When Cain brought his complete chaos into that physical environment, it reacted in such a way that there were no longer any controls over the state of disrepair into which it fell. Perhaps Cain was fundamentally changed into something we might call another species. His "mark" might well have been that his physical form was transformed so that he would be avoided by those who remained in Eden. It may also be true that animals of all sorts underwent significant, chaotic genetic changes that continued to evolve into many forms simply not seen in Eden. This would be consistent with the idea that creation was subjected to futility. Thus, many forms of life might well have existed for a time that ended when the universal flood occurred. Riotous "evolution" could occur in such a context rather than the gradual evolution we generally encounter in our educational system. In a sense, this hypothesis suggests significant genetic "damage" was incurred. This might explain why GOD was so incensed that the descendants of Seth would intermarry with the descendants of Cain. Ideas like this may be politically distorted to support ideas like ethnic cleansing. That is NOT the context of these comments. This discussion is reserved solely to a pre-flood context to deal with the issue of creatures such as dinosaurs.

CHAPTER FOUR

SIXTH DAY CONTINUES, PHASE TWO:

At the end of the previous chapter, we arrived at the point where everything that was to be created in the earth was finished. In the earliest days, all the elements to be used later in the creation cycle were put in place. Once that work was done, GOD used those early materials to create the more complex materials that are the stuff of life itself. Along the way, He also brought into being all the environmental components that would support life. Water, light, air, and ground (dirt, minerals), were in place and certain living things could arrive. Plant life, with its ability to support the lives of more animate beings, arrived next. Then there was water, light, air, ground, and food for the animate creatures soon to come.

Waterborne creatures were next in the order. When they arrived, certain foods in vegetable form were already available to them. Then came the airborne creatures, followed by the land-borne creatures other than man. The Creation was "pregnant" for the coming of man.

Before delving into the details of man's arrival, let's review briefly the three fundamental declarations from Chapter Zero (you may also refer back to Chapter Zero for their explanations):

1. **The Creation** is a **deliberate** and **purposeful** work of **The Creator.**

2. A **"holy nation"** is the **central purpose** of creation.

3. The primary *motivation* for God's acts of creation is *love*.

    a) **The love of God desired an *object* of that love in addition to the Son of God:**

    b) ***New* sons of God as *objects* of that love.**

The "holy nation" of sons of God could not come to be using walnuts or elephants as sons. The sons, in order to be sons, needed to have certain characteristics and capabilities that were not given to any other kind of creature, including walnuts and elephants – or even angels. In a sense, the "sons" who would compose the "holy nation" were the instances of the *prime purpose* of the acts of creation. Everything else in The Creation had its purpose as a subsidiary to that prime purpose. This brings us to a new declaration, with its corollaries:

1. God brought The Creation into being as the dwelling place for "sons."

    a) The "sons" were to be assembled into a "holy nation" in The Creation.

    b) The purpose for the "sons" transcends The Creation.

    c) The "sons" would represent God in and to The Creation.

This would be no typical creature, but an entirely unique creature unlike all other living things. This son-creature would be enabled like no other, and would have responsibility unlike any other. The enablement would be built in at the time of creation so that the responsibility could be fulfilled. This final creature (and its future generations) would be created to be "sons" of God and to show forth to all the rest of The Creation what it means to be a "son of God." In these "sons of God," The Creation would see an exact representation of God. This creature, in the aggregate sense, would rule The Creation with His full, authoritative commission. The text of Genesis 1:26-28 leaves little doubt that these assertions are accurate. These "sons of GOD" would have full dominion over the works of His hands and their rule would benefit The Creation as though He were present in that role Himself. In other words, the man was to be authorized as Viceroy for the Godhead. Let's discuss that.

The Man-Creature

The stage was thus set for the purposes of GOD to go forward to their absolute fulfillment. At this point I wish to emphasize that the language that follows in this discussion reflects that used in the biblical text. Man, when the word is used in isolation, refers to what we call mankind or human beings. I do this because it is the language used to translate the scripture most faithfully. I am aware of the potential for political sensitivity in the use of this language. However, our discussion surrounds scripture and is not political in nature. It is my position that the scriptural and political contexts are not compatible for this discussion.

GOD exhibits purpose in all that He does. Therefore, everything that He created or made in the first five and one-half days of the creation cycle was pointing toward something. That something was the creation of man. The text in the creation narrative generally is fairly cryptic. It deals with generalities such as "everything that creeps on the ground after its kind" (Gen. 1:25, partial) to refer to non-mammalian, land-based creatures. Consider the myriad of species included in that term (e.g., insects and so forth). But when it comes to man, a rather lengthy passage ensues.

The new creature, man, was to be endowed with great purpose. Interestingly, the manifold purpose with which man was to be endowed had both "spiritual" and "earthly" components. (This was not true for any other creature in the earth.) This means that the commission to be given to man would begin in The Eternal and be seen in the natural. So let's see what that commission was.

> *Then GOD said, "Let Us make man in Our image,*
> *according to Our likeness; and let them rule over the fish*
> *of the sea and over the birds of the sky and over the cattle*
> *and over all the earth, and over every creeping thing that*
> *creeps on the earth" (Genesis 1:26).*

GOD purposed to make man in His own *image*. He also purposed to make man in His own *likeness*. Actually, the text quotes GOD in His declaration, and the possessive pronoun used is "Our" rather than "His." Without discussion at this point, I will assert that the reason for the difference in person in the pronoun is found in the nature of the Godhead. GOD the Father and GOD the Son are both found in the Godhead and it was a collective will and intention that was being expressed in Genesis 1:26. The most likely case is that GOD the Father was speaking to GOD the Son in this passage.

To some, the use of the two expressions is simply a poetic redundancy. Careful reading, however, suggests an alternative way of viewing the matter. It appears that the two terms "image" and "likeness" actually refer to two aspects of man. Man was to exist in the image of the Godhead *and* in the likeness of the Godhead. This appears to be a more satisfactory reading than to assume a gloss of the two terms, image and likeness. At a very superficial level, if we were to assert that he was the image of someone else, we would assume the reference was to appearance. On the other hand, likeness more likely would refer to behavioral matters. In life we all often note how someone "looks like" another person or "behaves like" that other person, or both, and we well understand the distinction. I share certain physical characteristics with my late natural father. In some ways I could be described as acting like him as well. But the two things are different and not dependent on one another. Hence, the assertion that the image of GOD means one thing and the likeness of GOD means another.[1]

Whatever the full actuality of the meaning of "image" and "likeness," they both point to The Eternal. GOD's image exists first in The Eternal and GOD's likeness exists first in The Eternal. The fact that

GOD made man the way He did implies that He intended for man to "look like" and "act like" Himself whenever observed by others; in other words, the other entities that existed in The Creation. GOD must have intended for the entire non-human population of The Creation to observe how He made man in such a way that man would faithfully represent GOD to those observing the act. After this, the image and likeness of GOD would be observable in The Creation just as it was in The Eternal.[2] So, first of all, man was to represent the Godhead that exists in The Eternal to the rest of The Creation; the boundless Uncreated would be seen inside the confines of The Creation. I will be so bold as to suggest that the greatest proof of GOD was intended to be the man-creature. Man would be a more accurate representation of GOD than even the angels.

The Commission

The endowments that cause man to "point to" The Eternal connect this creature to The Eternal in a manner in which no other creature has been enabled to participate. In all of creation, GOD imparted His image and likeness to man alone. Not even the angels were so endowed. Having endowed man with the divine image and likeness, it then was necessary to commission man to his appropriate role. It is only in the context of fulfilling this role that behavior (likeness) can be observed.

Man was to rule or have dominion over that part of The Creation that we call the earth (Gen. 1:26). As the text progresses, various aspects of this commission are amplified, but the basic idea of "rule" is at the core. Obviously, this commission does not refer directly to The Eternal. The delineation of the subjects of man's rule makes this clear.

If we put together the parts of the narrative referring to man that relate to The Eternal and those that refer to The Creation, we easily conclude that man was to represent GOD in The Creation by ruling over its various aspects in the same way that GOD Himself would if He were ruling directly. If man's commission was to rule over the earth and its inhabitant entities as GOD would, then he needed the specific empowerment to do so. Without adequate power and authority, man could not fulfill his commission. He needed properties derived directly from The Eternal in order to rule effectively over his domain in The Creation.

To be clear, when GOD made man, He designed, authorized, empowered, and commissioned His newest and highest creation to rule as vice-regent over that part of The Creation that was positioned beneath the boundary between the atmosphere and outer space. This included all living things and the earth itself. It seems unreasonable to think that GOD would provide such a commission but not make the entire domain amenable to said dominion. It must be true then that the "earth" part of The Creation, by GOD's design, was pre-disposed to be ruled by man.

The "heavens" part of The Creation was not included in man's commission (Gen. 1:26-28), and therefore would not be pre-disposed to be ruled by man, at least not in this age. Having described the opening acts of creation (Gen. 1:1-8) and the deploying of the luminary bodies (Gen. 1:14-18), the creation narrative is essentially silent on matters having to do with the heavens. This is entirely reasonable as the dominion of man is the primary concern of scripture (Gen. 1:26).[3]

The "Viceroy"

We must make sure we use the term viceroy (or vice-regent) in a proper and consistent manner. Because this term is not widely used in modern times, it needs clarification. Its use in this book is somewhat limited but is consistent with typical definitions. Let's consider a few of the key ideas associated with the term "viceroy."

Typically, in presidential democracies, a person is selected, usually by election, to serve as second in authority to the president. This office provides for immediate succession in the event the president is incapacitated. This vice-president steps into the presidency, either temporarily or permanently depending on the circumstances behind the succession. By the nature of the office, the vice-president inherently possesses the same authority as the president, but only in trust.

Short of actually succeeding the president, a vice president sometimes exercises his latent authority as a substitute for the president when so delegated by the president, such as in high profile ceremonial events or situations requiring presidential authority for their execution, but which do not require the actual physical presence of the president. When representing the president on such occasions, the vice president's words and actions carry the same authority as the president's.

Monarchial systems differ somewhat from democracies in their operations. In monarchial systems, prime authority is reserved solely for the monarch. Whether there is someone to temporarily substitute for the monarch is up to the monarch. It is not absolutely necessary that there be such a person. As the need arises, a monarch may make one-time, temporary appointments of a limited kind in order to get done those things democracies consider ordinary for a vice-president. In other words, the monarch might commission some particular person to perform a specific task for the crown with the full weight and authority of the crown behind the person so commissioned, but limited to the parameters of that commission.

Most modern monarchies are "hybrids" known as "constitutional monarchies" because they contain significant elements of democracy. For example, the designee for most activities is elected by the people rather than appointed by the monarch, and thus serves for a specific period of time according to the terms of office. While this arrangement dilutes the power of the monarch, it keeps the power of the people in sight. A constitutional monarchy is a hybrid in the sense that it combines a hierarchical system where accession to the throne is determined by birth or the will of the monarch with a democratically elected body headed by a prime minister tasked with carrying out ordinary affairs of state.

Prior to modern times, monarchs frequently found it desirable to appoint a highly trusted person (often, but not always, a relative) to oversee the ordinary work of government and keep the state running in a consistent and efficient manner. This highly trusted person would carry out the will of the monarch with respect to state matters on an ongoing basis, and was accorded the same deference, respect, and obedience as if the monarch was personally present. Such a person exercised functions and powers similar to those of a vice-president. But where a monarchy is involved, a more appropriate term for this office is "viceroy" ("roy" coming from the French *roi*, which means "king"). A viceroy, then, is a vice-monarch, or a vice-king, or a vice-regent, depending on the point of view.

Pharaoh and Joseph

The viceroy is commissioned by the monarch to operate on behalf of the monarch with delegated authority that may be very limited in scope or virtually unlimited. For example, the Pharaoh empowered Joseph to rule Egypt with very few restrictions on his authority (Gen. 41:38-45). Pharaoh's clear intent was that all Egypt would know that when Joseph spoke it was as though Pharaoh had spoken. Obviously, such a commission requires tremendous confidence on the part of the monarch, as well as his strict endorsement. By implication, Joseph's commission may have included authority in foreign affairs and the waging of war. Joseph's power was virtually complete and it was made well known in Egypt by virtue of Pharaoh's actions. Joseph's position certainly satisfies the definition of a viceroy, as his authority was virtually unlimited. There were other officials who had specific responsibilities and offices, but all of them were subject to Joseph's decisions and approval. Only the king (Pharaoh) had authority over him. Joseph, in turn, had authority over all other officials of the state.

Let's be clear. In terms of whatever pertained to Egypt, the Pharaoh possessed ultimate authority and power (as permitted by GOD, of course). Therefore, the Pharaoh possessed the right to distribute political authority and power as he chose within the context of Egypt. Of course, he was careful to make such distributions in a manner that protected his own interests, particularly the throne. In Joseph's case it appears the Pharaoh left the entire government of Egypt in Joseph's hands. This "vice-Pharaoh" (not a real term) was free to do what he wanted in the conduct of the public affairs of the nation. He was trusted to act exactly as Pharaoh desired.

The relationship between Joseph and Pharaoh is probably the most well-known picture for people today of how a monarch and a viceroy (vice-monarch) co-existed. This example can go a long way toward enabling us to understand what a viceroy is in relation to a monarch. So let's apply this paradigm to examine the commissioning of man.

Viceroy Adam

GOD's instructions in Genesis 1:26 commissioned the whole of mankind, but at the time of issuance it pertained to only one man, Adam.[4]

> *Then God said, "Let Us make man in Our image, according to Our likeness; and let them **rule** over the fish of the sea and over the birds of the sky and over the cattle and over all the earth, and over every creeping thing that creeps on the earth." God created man in His own image, in the image of God He created him; male and female He created them. God blessed them; and God said to them, "Be fruitful and multiply, and fill the earth, and **subdue** it; and **rule** over the fish of the sea and over the birds of the sky and over every living thing that moves on the earth"* (Genesis 1:26-28, emphasis added).

We may infer from the text here that it was necessary (at least from GOD's point of view) that man be made in the image and likeness of GOD in order for him to be appointed viceroy. GOD designed man not only to *be* the viceroy to the earth (including the seas and the atmosphere), but also designed him to have the capacity to perform those functions as GOD would. Furthermore, we may infer that GOD made it known to The Creation, at least the earth, that this was so, just as Pharaoh made it clear to all Egypt that Joseph was his vice-monarch (viceroy). Man was to be the viceroy of GOD insofar as the earth was concerned.

The Creation was mostly non-sentient. Therefore, it was necessary that GOD "announce" the viceroy as Pharaoh was later to announce the appointment of Joseph. In so doing, He placed the knowledge of that appointment into the very fabric of The Creation.[5] As He was bringing forth The Creation during the acts of creation, the "knowledge" that GOD was its king and that man was His viceroy was built in. There seems to be little doubt that even "the heavens" knew that man was viceroy to GOD in the earth. When the first man came to life, the whole of creation knew that he was the viceroy of GOD. It was not only in the nature of man; it was in the nature of the earth.[6]

In His *Image*

One of the issues that we cannot fully resolve is the matter of what is meant by the term "in Our image" (Gen. 1:26). Unless we conclude that "image" and "likeness" mean virtually the same thing, we simply have more difficulty thinking about image than we do likeness in this context. In other words, what does it mean to "look like" GOD?

GOD is Spirit (Jn. 4:24) and man is partially spirit. Certainly, this is part of the meaning of the image of GOD. Man alone, of all the creatures on earth, is a spiritual being. Man, composed of spirit covered over with a garment made of dirt, was made to be different than the other creatures in that dimension. No other living thing possesses the presence of the Spirit of GOD as a component of its being; only man.

The New Testament tells us that Adam was the *son* of GOD (Lk. 3:38). JESUS was the *only begotten Son* of GOD (Jn. 3:16). By adoption, we are sons of GOD (Rom. 8:15). No animal or plant is called a son of GOD, even by way of adoption. In the world we may often observe that a son "looks like" his father. That is often the case to a remarkable degree, even when the son and the father are completely estranged.

The biological impact of the one on the other is often undeniable and permanent. In such cases, the son **looks like** his father regardless of how either of them acts.

Another clue to the meaning of the term "*in Our image*" is provided by the pronoun itself. GOD must be speaking for the Godhead in this command. "Our image" likely refers to the image of the Godhead. The Godhead is, in some sense, a corporate entity. This man-creature was created in a corporate context (Gen. 1:27). The male and female were created together. Chapter 2 of Genesis is primarily an amplification of this fact. Just as the Godhead is more than just GOD the Father or GOD the Son, so it is with man. Initially, GOD placed the woman in the man at the time of creation. He then took the woman out of the man and united them into a corporate identity. This *corporeity* is another manifestation of the "image" of GOD.

In His *Likeness*

Likeness refers to the mode of being one exhibits. A person may be said to *act like* another person. This means that the one person exhibits behaviors that resemble those of the other person. In the present case, GOD had said He would make man "*in Our likeness*" (Gen. 1:26) as well as in His image. For the moment, let's assume that likeness refers to **acting like** in contrast to looking like.

In the last section we addressed the use of plural pronouns in the current biblical text. "Our" is obviously plural. It is, then, in reference to the Godhead. The man-creature was to resemble the Godhead in his behavior. Total harmony exists within the Godhead. Thus, we would expect that GOD the Father and GOD the Son are much alike in their behavioral comportment. Similarly, the man-creature, in *likeness*, would *act like* the Father and the Son.[7]

We can take two different approaches when considering the likeness of GOD that He built into the man-creature, and both probably apply. Remember, our emphasis here is on *acting like* GOD. The first one involves a prophetic utterance in Isaiah describing the coming of

GOD the Son that specifies that the Spirit of the Lord would rest on the coming Messiah. This presence of the Holy Spirit would result in certain behavioral traits the Messiah would exhibit, stated as properties He would possess. As a result of the presence of the Spirit in the life of the Messiah, He would exhibit godly wisdom, understanding, and so forth:

> *Then a shoot will spring from the stem of Jesse, And a branch from his roots will bear fruit. The Spirit of the* LORD WILL REST ON HIM, THE SPIRIT OF WISDOM AND UN- DERSTANDING, THE SPIRIT OF COUNSEL AND STRENGTH, THE SPIRIT OF KNOWLEDGE AND THE FEAR OF THE LORD. AND HE WILL DELIGHT IN THE FEAR OF THE LORD (Isaiah 11:1-3).

We made the point above that the man-creature, appointed as the viceroy of the Godhead, was relationally a son of GOD. As we know, the Messiah is the only begotten Son of GOD. He is the Firstborn. It seems quite reasonable that this human viceroy would bear this same Spirit of GOD. The human viceroy would then behave just as would the Firstborn.

The second dimension of "looking like" GOD can be found in what we call the fruits of the Spirit (Gal. 5:22-23). The man-creature, as we know, failed at being the viceroy of the Godhead. In Man's fallen state it became necessary for the Spirit of GOD to restore these behavioral characteristics to Man in the process of his restoration after the cross. This is the apparent meaning of "fruits of the Spirit" in the passage. The Spirit of GOD is about the business of causing those who will to bear these behavioral fruits. These "fruits" are, in some sense, a kind of personality profile of GOD. When a human person is enabled to bear these fruits of the same kind, that person will begin to "act" like GOD in his dealings with The Creation, particularly with other people, of course.

So when the Spirit of the Lord rests on us, that same Spirit pro- duces behavioral fruits in our lives that enable us to act like GOD. This picture, paired with the factors that define the "image" of GOD, provide a profile of the creature who would be qualified to be GOD's viceroy to The Creation.

Life experience teaches us that Man is not like that. Man, as we know ourselves, just does not exhibit this profile of image and likeness features. Regardless of that, this seems to have been the intent of the Creator when He made Man. What is the difference between what we see and the "design specifications?" That question will be taken up in a later chapter of this book.

For now, let's just accept that the profile does represent the intention of GOD when He made Man. If that is the case, then the man should have come into being with exactly those design features. GOD's declaration at the end of Sixth Day indicates that the man He made met the criteria in the design features. He judged The Creation to be "very good" as He finished His work (Gen. 1:31). It does not seem feasible then to assume that the man was any other than what He had intended. Otherwise, He would not have placed such a high value on His works. Had the man fallen short of the standards, it could not be the case that GOD would have been pleased. Not only was He pleased but His evaluation at the end of the creation narrative was of a higher order than His evaluation of the various stages of the process. Before this summary evaluation, He had found several other things to be "good." Now He found the final product to be "very good." It is not unreasonable to assume this was because He was quite pleased with the man-creature He had made.

Creation Conclusions

At the beginning of the creation narrative, we see GOD bringing into being a phenomenon we are calling The Creation. He brought The Creation into being to suit His own sovereign purposes. Our premise is that the prime purpose of The Creation was that GOD desired to have sons to love and to experience their love in return. This would demonstrate His being to the whole of The Creation. Because He so loved the creature He created to exist in sonship, He purposed that Man would rule the very creation which had been made to be the abode of Man. Because all authority has its source in GOD within The Eternal,[8] it was necessary that He delegate Man to rule in The Creation. Man was to rule the earth and all that pertains to the earth as a viceroy of GOD Himself. Because of this, it was necessary that Man be created in such a way that he bore the image and likeness of GOD. At the end of the creation narrative, it appears that all of GOD's purposes were met. Thus, He declared that the whole production, The Creation, was **very good**. He was pleased with it, so it must have been what He intended when He began the acts of creation.

The second chapter of Genesis provides us with an "expanded" view of the creation of Man. As Man was the pinnacle creation, this seems reasonable. In the expanded view, we will find more detail to help us understand this key event, the making of Man in the Image and Likeness of the Godhead.

After GOD created Man, He rested. His rest marked the end of His acts of creation. On that day, called the Sabbath, He had put into motion all that was required for the habitation of the new entities with which He so desired to enter into a love relationship.

---

[1] It is not reasonable to attempt absolutely to separate the two terms "image" and "likeness." In fact, efforts to do so result in each being used to explain the other. We call that "semantic overlap." However, in this discussion, we will try to focus on a common sense difference in which we may say "image" is related to "looks like" and "likeness" means "acts like." In this sense, it is likely that "corporeity" is a dimension of the "image" of GOD. At the same time, "corporeity" may well be reflected in some of the behaviors of GOD and of His sons.

[2] This would be the case in The Creation. The earth AND the heavens would be witnesses that the new creature bore the image and likeness of GOD. The Eternal, of course, also saw this. According to Genesis 1:31, GOD was very pleased with the work He had done.

[3] Third Heaven is explicitly the dominion of GOD. There is no hint in scripture that man is to exercise dominion either in First or Second Heaven. I think we could safely assume that the dominion of those two belongs to GOD as well. Revelation 2:26-27 speaks of our rule of the nations, by implication those of the earth, not those of heaven, as "nation" seems to be an earthly phenomenon.

[4] The first instance of this dominion was vested in Adam. It was subsequently vested in Seth and down through the generations to Melchizedek and, finally, to JESUS in a priesthood. In the earliest days, it seems there was one special priest in each generation. By the time Israel became a nation, GOD wanted the whole nation to exercise that dominion on His behalf. This seems to be the sense of the nation specified in Revelation 5:10.

⁵ The announcement of the dominion to be entrusted to man was likely the cause of the fall of Satan. When that became known, Satan could not tolerate that he would be eventually of lower rank than the frail earth creature. This animosity was like lead in his being and caused him to fall from Third Heaven to Second Heaven. This all seems to have happened when GOD commanded the man to have dominion (Gen. 1:28).

⁶ Romans 8:19-22 implies that the creation misses its viceroy and longs for it to return. The Creation needs for the ruler of the earth to be found again.

⁷ See chapter 5 of C. Gaulden, *Birth of The Holy Nation, volume 1*, (Chambersburg, PA: eGen, 2015) for a full discussion of the relationship between GOD the Father and GOD the Son as a model for human comportment. After all, The Creation knows how this ought to look.

⁸ See chapter two of C. Gaulden, *The Nature and Character of GOD*, (Chambersburg, PA, eGen, 2016) for a detailed discussion of the auto-generation of GOD's authority.

CHAPTER FIVE

THE VICEROY

In the previous chapter I argued that Man was created at the apogee of creation and that he was designed to be the ruler of The Creation, which was, in turn, created to be his home. We spent a great deal of that discussion focused on the "design features" of Man. The design of Man was quite a bit more complex than that of the other living beings in The Creation. Our goal now is to look into the making of Man in greater detail.

> *Now no shrub of the field was yet in the earth, and no plant of the field had yet sprouted, for the LORD GOD HAD NOT SENT RAIN UPON THE EARTH, AND THERE WAS NO MAN TO CULTIVATE THE GROUND. BUT A MIST USED TO RISE FROM THE EARTH AND WATER THE WHOLE SURFACE OF THE GROUND* (Genesis 2:5-6).

Interestingly, the text we are now focusing on opens with a reca- pitulation of the creation of food, describing certain conditions that existed before the creation of Man. Specifically, the text states that food plants were not yet producing food and that there was no rain. Rather than rain, GOD seems to have caused the land to be watered by some sort of reflux process that occurred at night. These rather interesting agricultural observations appear in the text (Gen. 2:5-6) just before the

93

operational description of the making of Man. It is to that portion of the narrative that we will now turn our attention.

"Of Dust from the Ground"

When GOD came around to the making of Man during Sixth Day, He set about it in what looks at first like a very odd manner. This creature, designed with the attributes of GOD, was to be created from inanimate material of the lowest form. The "highest" order of creature on the earth was to be made from its most humble substance insofar as the flesh was concerned. This least of substances would become the *biological habitation* for a creature whose primary attributes are the "image and likeness" of GOD. I can't stress enough the contrast found in that peculiar set of divine decisions.

It seems that GOD created other creatures from the ground (Gen. 2:19),[1] and used the same or similar material for making Man, who was the highest and most GOD-like of all the creatures in earth or in the heavens.[2] But the real innovation was the source of the life in Man. The other living creatures were given life in some manner, but Man was given life in a unique manner. Man was the only creature given life through the mechanism of the breath of GOD. He breathed life into the dust of the ground, and the first man came to be. It was the "breath of GOD" that was the source of that life. The life force was not in the dust from which his natural body was made. It was the Spirit of GOD imparted into the dust that was the force of life. The presence of the Spirit made that natural body particularly open to the ministrations of the Spirit in terms of the maintenance of the "image and likeness" of GOD that was to become the key component of Man. In other words, by seeing to it that the source of life in Man was the breath of GOD, GOD saw to it that Man was given every opportunity to be GOD-like in his life.[3]

Modern science tells us that man is a species of the mammalian group of animals. In the typical explanation of this modern view, man is not fundamentally different from other animals of similar physical structure. This appealing argument stresses the biology of man without any reference at all to the spiritual aspects of man. By contrast, it also makes no statement to the effect that "other" animals have spirits. Rather, if pressed, the priests of modern biology will deny there is any such thing as a spiritual entity. In so doing, they reduce Man to something that is not all that different from certain higher-order animals. The reasoning sentience of man, in this scheme, is simply a result of some evolutionary accident that persisted because it provided the "species" with superior properties of some sort.

Man is not simply another species of mammal. While Man does possess many physical traits with some groups of mammals, those mammals do not possess the presence of the breath of GOD. The presence of the Spirit of GOD is not in them. This distinction is of prime importance because it is what links man to The Eternal as sons of GOD. It is more than just a matter of flesh and blood. It is a matter of spirit, and not just any spirit. It is a matter of the Spirit of GOD. In scripture, Man is not an evolutionary event; he is a purposed product of the direct work of the Godhead to provide a ruler for the earth-components of The Creation.

If we assume the scripture is the narrative presentation of the work of GOD in The Creation, it does not seem reasonable to conclude that Man is the end-product of a blind evolutionary process. Such a process has no goal; nor has it controls to guide it. The cosmogony of scripture has an intelligent and all-powerful GOD to guide it. To be clear, the argument is not that there is nothing that looks like evolution, but that blind evolution is not reasonable for a Creator who has such a high purpose for The Creation, particularly Man. To leave to chance that Man would eventually come out of an unguided process of trial and error is just not consistent with what we have presented as the power-driven purposes of GOD.

In short, this dusty creature was exactly as GOD intended. We shall tend later to the current status of Man. For now, let's just understand that Man has a high purpose and is the very delight of GOD. Even though He housed Man in a body of dust, He placed in Man the essence of His own being. He purposed Man to be that creature that linked The Creation to The Eternal.

The Commission

Having designed Man to be His own key delight in The Creation, GOD inserted that being into the humblest of substances in order to insert him into The Creation. Let's return now to the purpose behind Man's design.

Man was intended and designed to rule in the earthly region of The Creation as the viceroy of GOD. Man's very design included the enabling for exercising that dominion. Even more significantly, Man's prime purpose in GOD's plan was to be sons of GOD in essentially the same sense that GOD the Son was a son of GOD the Father. GOD installed all the necessary properties at creation. Remember, though, that GOD also reasoned that the son should choose to reciprocate the love of the Father for the son. In order to do that, you recall, it was necessary that Man choose to do so. To so choose would demonstrate authentic love. But having the capacity to choose to reciprocate GOD's love, as a true son of GOD would do, requires the equal capacity to choose not to reciprocate that love and therefore choose not to be a true son of GOD. A son would be qualified to be viceroy IF he chose to be a true son of GOD. If he chose to be a not-son, he would not be qualified to be the viceroy. This decision was not to be made in a vacuum. The default state of Man was the viceroy state. In a sense, before the decision was made, Man was to live in the "son" state.

Consider the risk GOD was taking. Were He not omniscient and omnipotent, He would certainly be holding His breath even as He brought that first man to life. Even considering the outcome of the decisions of the first man, it appears that GOD must have been cosmically excited as the moment of life came to the first man. Now His work of creation would culminate in its highest work and be finished. When the first man received his life, he became the viceroy of the dominion which had been created for just such a ruler as he.[4] In the same instant, the cosmos received the one who would rule it as the Creator would have ruled it: the viceroy. The Creation must also have rejoiced in that moment.

The viceroy came to life and assumed his vice-regnal activities at the same time. He was created a mature man. He did not arrive as a baby who needed to grow into manhood. He was a grown man from the outset.[5] Furthermore, when this first man began to breathe on his own, he had within his frame all the power and expertise required to be the viceroy. Human history had begun, and with it the saga of the relationship of the Father with the intended son. From that moment, that Father-son saga became the focus of scripture.

The first task in the rule of the brand new viceroy was to name the animals who were brought to him by his Father (Gen. 2:19-20). This initiated his relationship with animate creatures. Because he was the viceroy, GOD respected the results of his activity. By the way, the animals came to him to be named. He did not have to go find them. That is certainly consistent with the idea of ruling. Somehow the animals knew to go to him to be named. This is another evidence of a kind of intelligence that pervaded the components of The Creation.

The Suitable Helper

We cannot know why GOD decided that Adam needed a helper, but He did. The text implies that the animal naming process revealed that fact, but it seems it was known by the Creator to begin with. But let's back up a bit. When GOD announced that He would make Man in His image and likeness, the text goes on to say, "male and female, He created them" (Gen. 1:27). The key word here is "them." This is curious wording in that the immediately preceding phrase is, "in the image of God He created him." In the same act, apparently, He created both "him" and "them." This implies that "him" and "them" are the same thing. This can only be true in one way: the "him" must also in some sense be "them." In other words, the man was both singular and plural. In turn, this must mean the man was corporate. In the man there were both a male and a female.

The "suitable helper" (Gen. 2:18) was already within the man in some sense.[6] The search seems to have been conducted to verify for the man that the suitable helper would not come from any of the other created things.[7] None of them could qualify as "suitable" no matter how helpful one of them might be. They were unsuitable as the man's "suitable helper" because they had not been created as the man had been created, with the indwelling activity of the Spirit. Lacking that essential quality, they never could become qualified, and there was no reason to expect they would. The work of creation was over. Only another entity with the same spiritual properties as the man could be a suitable helper for the man.

The description of GOD's activities on Sixth Day implied a corporate identity in the man He created. If there were, in a sense, two persons in that entity, they would be quite similar to one another. For example, as a scientific matter, they would need to have the same DNA. The text of Genesis 1:27 strongly implies just that. There were at least two in the one, one of each, male and female. THEY were the corporate product of the making of man in the image and likeness of GOD. The male and the female were created simultaneously within the single context of the male body made "of dust from the ground" (Gen. 2:7).

Man, the singular phenomenon, was found by GOD (and arguably by the man himself) to need a helper. All other living things were found (both by GOD and the man) to be inadequate to be suitable helpers. Once this fact was firmly established, it was time to bring the female forth from "within" the male to be his suitable helper and companion. Only this female, of all the living entities in The Creation, was suitable.

Because the female was to come forth from the flesh of the man, she would also have already in her the presence of the same Spirit as that found in the man. She was, then, of the same character as the man. In some sense, she had the same capabilities as the man. We may infer that they were very much alike, and yet enough difference existed between them to make them distinct from one another. Their companionship would have two main characteristics: being alike in that they each bore the image and character of GOD, and being different in their flesh.

Their *similarity* (really sameness) in the Spirit made them capable of perfect companionship in the matters of their vice-regal appointment.[8] Their *difference* in the flesh provided the platform for the union to come.

The method by which the female was extracted from the male is very interesting. Something much like surgery occurred. Some physical material was taken out of the man. The word that is typically translated "rib" in this passage occurs fifty-two times in scripture but is translated as "rib" only twice. The idea that the part removed was a rib is not unacceptable, but its use may limit our understanding of the content of the passage. *Something* was taken from the living flesh of the man. That *something* was living material. In it was the DNA of the man. Out of that living flesh, GOD made a woman. Out of that incomplete part an entire, other living entity was made. The loss of it was not harmful to the man. This was not customary. The living entity that came forth was apparently a *mature* woman insofar as the flesh was concerned. This, then, was not birth as we know it. In fact, it was a unique event in all of human history. Furthermore, the female came forth as an adult, not as a child needing to be raised. She was ready to undertake her "duties."[9] We can understand that this new person who came into being was not born in the sense that the rest of us have been born.[10] This woman was, in a sense, "born" from the man and not of a woman. She was "of" his flesh just as we are "of" the flesh of our natural parents. She came "out of" him just as a child comes forth from the womb of the mother and contains properties of the flesh that come from both of the parents. In this case, Eve was a fully-grown child whose "mother" was also her father. This first instance of human "birth" involved neither two parents nor the womb of a woman. There was no customary mixing of genes. Except in gender, she was a biological duplicate of the man unless GOD, in some unspecified manner, made her with different properties.

Let's remember that the man was still a completely qualified viceroy of GOD. There is no reason to doubt that the woman possessed the same spiritual attributes or that she too had the presence of the Spirit of

GOD to provide her with those attributes. Again, unless GOD changed these things in her in some unspecified way, she was like the man from whom she had been taken. The woman, then, was fully qualified to be the companion (suitable helper) of the viceroy. We might even argue that his exercise of his vice-regnal (ruling in the place of the king, by direct intention of the king) duties was incomplete until she was brought forth from him.

GOD was now entrusting the rule of the earth components of The Creation that He had created for them to these two perfect (faultless) people.[11] Perhaps they were to jointly perform the roles of the viceroy. At the same time, we do not wish to suggest there was in any way present anything in them that would lead to confusion in the prosecution of their roles.[12]

Whether the male could have continued to rule as viceroy alone is not given to us to know. There is no apparent reason that could not have occurred, but the property of the corporeity of the Godhead argues that this was the design of GOD to begin with. The bringing forth of the female took place after the creation narrative ended. However, she was in some sense built into the male at the time of creation. Provisionally, we may assert that there is a difference in the manner in which the personality of GOD manifests itself within The Creation when it comes to male and female. A kind of complementarity is implied, not a kind of competition.

Interestingly, the basic creation narrative ends at end of Sixth Day with the creation of the male. I have argued that the female was "within" the male at the time of creation, but was not uniquely or independently created at that time. After the male had been brought into the world, GOD decided that The Creation was "very good." At the time the creation cycle ended, there was only the male in the earth. The female was not yet present. She was not a feature of creation directly. Her introduction as a separate entity occurred after the six days of creation were over. It is likely to have occurred after that first Sabbath when GOD rested from creation. This too distinguishes the female from the male. His presence occurred before the end of Sixth Day. Her appearance seems to have been after the creation Sabbath. He was created during the work of creation. She was born in the time of GOD's rest.

Sabbath (Saturday, Abib 7)

Did the activities of rule to which GOD put the male begin on the Sabbath that ended creation week? It seems likely the answer is no. The argument for a break in the events is that eventually GOD commanded such a thing at Sinai (Ex. 20:8). Specifically, the amplification of the "remember" command forbad "ordinary" work on the Sabbath (Ex. 20:9-10). The man's ordinary work was to rule. There were certain matters to which the Lord was to turn His attention as the male began to rule. The text has a tone that indicates these things were "ordinary work." Therefore, because GOD rested from all His labors on that first Sabbath, we should feel some comfort that the male did not begin his ruling activities until Sunday, which was the second occurrence of Day One. The animals could wait another day for their names.

In fact, it is likely that the male was not fully installed until Eden was made. Genesis 2:8-14 describes some of the things GOD accomplished to set the stage for the man. Their order in the narrative argues that the man had been made before these actions were taken, but that is not necessarily the case. In any event, we find the making of Eden in them. GOD knew that He intended Eden to be the dwelling place for Man. Hence, we may argue that the making of Eden happened during the week of creation. The fact that Eden is such a specific phenomenon (as is the making of specific rivers) may explain its inclusion in chapter 2 rather than chapter 1 of Genesis. Eden was made ready for the man, along with the two special trees (life and knowledge) when we take up the story of the man. The exact wording of the passage, though, implies that Eden was under construction simultaneously with the making of the man so that as soon as he was created, he could be placed in the garden. In some sense that would be the end of GOD's labors.

In other words, the textual evidence suggests that the making of Eden, the planting of the two special trees in the garden, and the making of the four rivers took place at about the same time GOD was fashioning the man. The passage (Gen. 2:8-14) is an amplification of facts found in chapter 1 to provide some specifics. If this is true, then when GOD made the man, He immediately placed him in the garden in Eden. This seems the most likely scenario.

If those things are accurate, as seems to be the case, then the man was installed in the garden in Eden on Sixth Day. So when the Sabbath occurred, GOD rested and The Creation began to "operate."

After that Sabbath, on the second Day One (Sunday), Adam began to rule in The Creation. His first task as viceroy was to name the animals as GOD sent them to him. It was after this process that the decision to bring the female into the world took place. In some sense, Sabbath "separates" the male from the female. In the creation cycle everything necessary for the family life of the male and female had been put into place. A place had been prepared for her, but she was not yet in it. These things occurred before the Sabbath. When all was ready and GOD had entered His rest, she was brought forth from the "hiding place" in which she had been placed originally.[13]

"She Shall Be Called Woman"

After GOD had put into place everything necessary for the introduction of the woman prior to the first Sabbath, and the man had begun his dominion in the earth, GOD brought forth the female. From that time she would be the "suitable helper" for the male. It is interesting that the first thing Adam said when the two were "introduced" had nothing to do with her qualifications as a helper. He seems to have been focused on her appearance. It was that which he seems to have first noticed. He could have commented on her brawn or her intelligence, but he was drawn first to her appearance. At least we surmise that was the case. He "claimed" her from the perspective that she was indeed taken from him. The typical attraction a male feels for a female was at work. His claim was legitimate, but the text moves on right away to the bonding between the two of them, not her activities as suitable helper. Not only was she the "suitable helper," but the two of them became one flesh.

Before we move on to the happenings in Eden, let's deal with issues of timing. I contend (without proof) that the events after Adam began to name animals took place in a very short period of time. Perhaps only a few days, or even only a few hours, passed after the Sabbath before the "wedding" of the male and the female. We tend to see these things taking a lot of time, but there is no practical reason for that. It could be that the whole set of events leading up to the joining of the male and the female into one flesh took place in a day. That will remain unknown. I set the question before us here only to stimulate thought.

In the next chapter, we will return to the command GOD gave to the man regarding the fruit of the knowledge of good and evil to set up the discussion of what happened that resulted in the "breaking" of The Creation.

---

[1] Genesis 2:19 *could* be read to imply that man was created before animals, but that is not the case. The animals were *formed out of the ground*, which is like the creation of man except that the breath of GOD did not enter the animals. Thus, whatever souls animals might have are not the same as the souls of humans. Whether animals have souls is an open question in my opinion because of our deficient knowledge of what constitutes a soul. For example, "soul" is probably not instinct.

[2] GOD-likeness was given to man alone. It was not given to the animals. "What is man that thou art mindful of him?" (Psalm 8:4 KJV). Man is even to be superior to the angels according to Hebrews 2:6-8, at least in our position "in" CHRIST.

[3] The indwelling Spirit of GOD is given to us alone of all creatures. It is this Spirit who gives life even to our mortal bodies (Rom. 8:11). This is no small thing, as the Spirit of GOD knows the mind of GOD so that men may know what the mind of GOD is (Rom. 8:26-27).

[4] For this, GOD the Son was slain from the creation, that these sons of GOD would be made worthy of the trust that leads to their actualization as sons. GOD the Son was the surety or guarantee that GOD the Father would have mature sons in The Creation.

[5] The Creation came into being in a mature state. By this I mean, trees were created ready to bear fruit. Grasses were ready to bear grain. Foxes were created ready to breed young. The man came as *huios* at the time of his creation. He was not a *nepios* needing to grow up, as we are. We are children first, in the flesh and in the spirit, while we grow into the adult state. At least we are enabled to do so if we will.

[6] This "helper" would be of the same kind. She would be appropriate and complementary. The two of them were to complete one another, not compete with one another. They were to be first instance of the corporeity GOD was installing in the earth.

[7] Revelation 5 contains a scene in which an "appropriate" entity was needed to open the seals of the book. Not just anyone would do. The opener of the book was as important as the contents of the book. The helper was as important as the man.

[8] Spiritually they were the same, as "in Christ there is neither male nor female" (Gal. 3:8). In the flesh, however, there was a complementary difference that permitted their bonding and reproduction. In that, government and order are also found.

[9] The male was "pregnant" with a full-grown female at the time he was created. Adam "gave birth" to a full-grown woman. This was a singular event in every way. When GOD removed her from Adam, she was ready to be his full partner and wife.

[10] It was not possible for Eve to be born as we are, there being yet no female womb from which she could come forth. Her "birth" was unique, as was the birth of JESUS. In His case no male was involved. In hers, no female was involved. These two unique cases were necessary for the full unfolding of the will of GOD. Neither of them has ever again been necessary.

[11] In this case, "perfect" means there was nothing yet wrong with them. They had not failed GOD in any way. They were not perfect as GOD is, but the potential was there for them to lead blameless lives so that they would have a *real choice* in failing to lead blameless lives.

[12] The male had begun the processes of rule before the female was taken from him. This was in the naming of the animals. There is an implication he had finished that work before she was brought forth from him. Each animal had been evaluated and found inadequate. Hence, each animal was probably already named. This might suggest the role of leader for the male and the role of suitable helper for the female. Just as GOD the Father exercised primacy over GOD the Son, the man seems to have been made to exercise a kind of primacy, being first in the manifestation in creation. Primacy gives rise to proper exercise of authority, as in the Godhead.

[13] We too are hidden in CHRIST (Col. 3:3), that we might be revealed later (Col. 3:4) in the fullness of His glory.

CHAPTER SIX

THE "BREAKING" OF CREATION

Adam and Eve were the crowning achievement of GOD's acts of creation. He placed them into a creation that had no flaws. Insofar as The Creation was concerned, they themselves were flawless, being made in the image and likeness of GOD.[1] Eden was planted. The tree of life and the **tree of the knowledge of good and evil** were in the garden that was in Eden. GOD had issued to the man the command to not eat the fruit of the **tree of the knowledge of good and evil**. Adam's rule had begun with the naming of the animals. The woman had been brought forth as the first production of GOD *after* the creation cycle. A marriage had ensued. This is the setting for understanding the events in the garden that led to the breaking of The Creation.

We established earlier that GOD determined before He began the acts of creation, to provide Man with the amazing, unparalleled opportunity to truly be a son of GOD by his own choice. GOD did not organize things so that Man had to crawl up out of some ditch to choose to be a son of GOD. Instead, He installed the first man fully in the place of the son and viceroy of GOD. The choice Adam was about to face had nothing to do with saving himself, but *maintaining his status* as the son and viceroy of GOD. That status was his to lose, not his to gain. This is an important truth. The only way Adam could lose was by exercising his choice to take a not-son course of action. Had he not chosen the path of not-son, the outcome would have been very different. We also know that GOD, in His perfect and eternal counsel, understood the risks inherent in the choices available to the man and provided, before the acts of creation began, the principle and method of redemption from the wrong choices Adam eventually made.[2] So let's get into that.

On the day GOD created the man, He placed him in a garden planted in the east of Eden. This appears to have been on Sixth Day, and appears to be *the last act* of creation.[3] Let's keep in mind that the woman was *hidden in* the man at that time (Col. 3:3; Phil. 3:9), and that her introduction later was not a separate creation, but a "birth" into the already operating creation. The operational aspect of the man's rule began with the naming of the animals. Then came the "birth" of the woman. Perhaps that was the first "birth." In that sense, *the man was a creation* and *the woman was a kind of "first fruit"* of The Creation. It is not that she was not created, but that *she was hidden in the other* human who was created until the time came for her to be revealed. This reminds us that we are hidden with (in) CHRIST (Col. 3:3). The hiddenness of the woman suited the purposes of GOD in the revelation of Himself within The Creation after it had been created. The man could not be hidden because he had to be in place when the creation narrative came to an end. Otherwise, there would be no ruler when the time came. The Creation was not designed to rule itself. The viceroy was a necessity in the wisdom and plan of GOD.

In the Garden

In some particular place in the earth, the Lord established a locale called Eden. Within that locale, He established a garden; scripture says He "planted" it. Planting is an interesting way to see the thing. He seems to have done this on Sixth Day at about the same time He was making Man. It seems that the Lord made Eden specifically for the man. Within the context of Eden, the easterly garden was to be the actual habitat of the man. The man was to rule over the earth and all living things in the earth. Apparently, he was to accomplish this from the garden. In a sense, the garden was to be the focal location of his vice-regal activities. Those components of The Creation which had to do with the earth would come to him for his declarations. Metaphorically, there was a vice-regal "throne" in the garden that reflected the throne of GOD in Third Heaven.

We cannot with certainty describe what it was about Eden that made it different from the rest of the earth, only that it received particular attention in its making. There was no political purpose to be served in its separation from the rest of the land on the earth. Perhaps it was a particularly lush area in terms of its plant growth. Perhaps it was simply centrally located in the lone continent. Whatever the reason, Eden was in the earth and was a specific part of the landmass of the earth. On a map of the earth at that time (had there been one), we might see an area called Eden surrounded by the rest of the land that we might call Not-Eden.

We do know that Eden was "in the east," but that is all the locational help we get.[4] The Creation no doubt "knew" that Eden was the main feature of the land area.[5] In the well-ordered creation, which was perfect in its making, this area would have been considered special. In some sense, Eden was a "holy place" because GOD had lavished special attention on it by singling it out. By so doing, the Creator designated it as a holy place in advance.

If Eden is a figurative holy place, then we might think of the garden of Eden as the "holy of holies" because GOD specifically planted the garden in Eden.[6] From this "holy of holies" the man would rule as viceroy in the earth. Of course, these are metaphors. Even so, they are worthy of careful consideration because they reveal something of the mindset and manner of GOD. He was very deliberate, however casually we may read the account.

The garden, it appears, contained every useful kind of plant. If the plant appeared elsewhere in the earth, it also appeared in the garden in Eden. The garden in Eden, though, received two plants (trees) that occurred nowhere else in The Creation. We cannot know for sure, but the text implies that these two trees were unrelated to all the other plants God had created. We may infer that they were not related to one another either, except in their physical proximity. They each appeared singularly and apparently without the capacity for reproduction. The first of these two trees mentioned is the "tree of life."[7] From initial inspection, we may infer that the fruit of that tree was a source of life to be consumed by already living beings. Whatever life came from that fruit, then, was not limited to the biological life, as we think of it, already possessed by the living being. In fact, the text later reveals that the life that came from consumption of that fruit was eternal life, not the temporary life that characterizes living beings in The Creation.[8] So the narrative shifts its focus to this garden in the eastern part of Eden. Let's examine what we know of the other tree.

"Did God Really Say?"

Although most Bible translations do not frame the question quite this way, it does capture the essence of what the serpent asked the woman. It is not likely that the serpent was confused. On the contrary, it is safe to assume that the serpent knew precisely the instructions God had given to the man when He created him and set him in the garden. His attempt here was to engage the woman in dialogue designed to trap her. Of course, we know that he was successful in this venture.

Who was this "serpent?" Our typical inclination is to infer that the word "serpent" means the same thing as the modern word "snake." Insofar as the English language is concerned, this is true. In that sense, "serpent" is an archaic word for "snake." What is interesting is to ask ourselves whether there is some deeper meaning in the appearance of this particular creature. Why not a mole or a peacock? Why was it a serpent who took on the role of the tempter in the narrative of the fall of Man?

The word serpent actually has a broader range of meanings beyond simply snake, including some almost metaphorical aspects that are associated with more sinister creatures.⁹ We cannot fully describe the serpent, but he is laden hereafter with particular fear and loathing. We will see in a later section that he is under a perpetual curse from the time of Eden.

The biblical text itself presents an important observation in the matter when it describes the serpent as more "crafty" than other animals (Gen. 3:1) The King James Version uses the word "subtil" (subtle) rather than "crafty." There was a way about the serpent that enabled him basically to persuade the woman using indirect reasoning.¹⁰ He used a carefully constructed question that contained a false accusation against GOD as the hook to draw her into conversation with him. His false accusation was based in a true fact: GOD had indeed commanded the man to avoid eating a particular fruit. What the serpent did was expand the context of that prohibition in such a way as to prompt the woman to make a "corrective" response, in defense of God, so to speak. The way he phrased the question, a simple response appeared inadequate to her. She had to correct his "error." It was in responding to the serpent's "bait" that she began down the path that soon would lead her to act in a manner contrary to the will of GOD.

For our consideration, the question actually contained two parts. First is the kernel of truth. There was one tree that bore forbidden fruit. Had the serpent asked the question, "Did GOD tell you not to eat the fruit of the tree of knowledge of good and evil?" her answer would have been "Yes." Had he followed that with the complementary question, "Did GOD tell you not to eat the fruit of any of the other trees?" she would have said "No." The text makes it clear that the serpent combined the two questions in such a way as to create the desired quandary for the woman. As most of us would, the woman separated out the first implied question when she answered. In doing so, she added a bit to the restriction, probably to highlight that her answer only referred to the one fruit. GOD had said not to eat that fruit. When the woman answered the serpent, she added that they were even forbidden to touch it. By her statement, to even touch that fruit would lead to death. She added the part about not even touching the fruit. At a minimum, she was clarifying for herself and for the serpent the distinction between this and all other fruits. Perhaps she even resented the restriction GOD had placed on eating the fruit, but we cannot know that for sure.

Some may ask whether the fruit was forbidden only to Man but not to all other creatures. Or perhaps they might ask why GOD would plant the tree if its fruit was to be forbidden. Most likely the fruit was planted as a one-of-a-kind to accomplish the purpose wrapped in the prohibition. If that is so, the fruit likely would not be attractive to creatures other than Man. The rest of the living creatures in the earth would know by virtue of the instinct GOD placed within them to avoid the fruit. They would have no reason, positive or negative, to know the difference between good and evil. In fact, we can easily argue that Man is the only creature with that knowledge. This leads us logically to the conclusion that only Man would be interested in the fruit and that it was planted (and forbidden) in order to provide the man and woman with a tangible object to either partake of or avoid, thus making the choice to be a son of GOD, or to be a not-son.

If it was not GOD's purpose that Man would eat the fruit that came from the **tree of the knowledge of good and evil**, we may propose that He did not design Man to have that knowledge. We, as creatures, were not intended to know the difference between good and evil. GOD gave the first man and woman the capacity to have that knowledge, but the knowledge was not built into them. Man could function properly as the viceroy of GOD without knowing the difference between good and evil. By extension, to be a fully functioning and mature son of GOD, it is not necessary to have that knowledge. The choice having been made by the first man and woman, though, we all are born needing to have this knowledge rather than an instinctual capacity to do only what is good. The properties that GOD placed in Man at the time of creation made Man not yet wicked. His state of un-marred-ness (in that he was made in the image and likeness of GOD with respect to the concerns of The Creation) was such that he would simply act as GOD would act in all things. This must be so because GOD had entrusted the earth and all that was in it into the hands of the first man as GOD's own viceroy.

Your Will

Had that particular tree not been planted in the garden in Eden, two things would be true. First, the man and woman would not have had a context for discovering their own willfulness, and, second, sin would not (yet) have had a doorway into the world. But *sin is not the point.* What really matters in the narrative is the relationship between GOD the King and His viceroy in the earth. That relationship was designed to reflect the relationship between GOD the Father and GOD the Son that already existed in The Eternal before The Creation came to be. That relationship had, and has, as one of its properties a complete harmony between the will of the Father and the response to that will on the part of the Son.[11] To mirror this relationship in the earth, in the sight of The Creation, it was necessary that the viceroy prefer the will of the Father *over his own will* in all things. Otherwise, he could not responsibly exercise his duties as viceroy. The "forbidden fruit" existed by the will of GOD in order to enable the man to choose whether or not to exercise *obedience in all things.* The exercise of obedience in all things requires also the capacity to not do so. The "forbidden" fruit existed only to provide the context for that kind of obedience. No other creature needed to make such a choice as no other creature was intended to be the viceroy of GOD the King. There was, then, a one-to-one relationship between Man and the tree that produced that fruit. That fruit, and consequently that tree, had no other purpose. The tree was the only mode through which the relationship between GOD and Man could be damaged.

This stands in contrast to the **tree of life**, which produces very specific benefits, as revealed in Revelation 21. The fruit of the **tree of the knowledge of good and evil** produced only death through a divinely undesirable dimension of knowledge so abhorrent to GOD that He would forbid and curse the coming of that knowledge into The Creation. By implication, the knowledge Man possessed before consuming the fruit was only a "knowledge of good." There was no evil or the knowledge of it.

When the woman interacted with the serpent that day, she distorted the command of GOD as well. Some would say this is quibbling; that her extension of the command to even touching the fruit was not a serious matter. In fact, they might go so far as to say that GOD might well have said or meant to say not to touch the fruit. It is unlikely that the original command included not touching the fruit, even though that would be a good idea if it was not to be eaten. It was the consumption that "opened" their eyes that was forbidden, not the existence of the fruit. GOD deliberately planted the tree that bore the fruit in the garden home He had prepared for them. It was unavoidable that they would come into contact with it. And it was in that contact that they would decide whether or not to fully and accurately represent the One who had created them and designed them to be His viceroy. Fully ruling would include ruling over the fruit they were forbidden to eat, not eating it but reflecting the full glory of GOD by eschewing its consumption.

The Conversation

Let's turn our attention now to the conversation between the serpent and the woman. We have already discussed it in part, but let's focus squarely on it at this point.

> *Now the serpent was more crafty than any beast of the field which the LORD God had made. And he said to the woman, "Indeed, has God said, 'You shall not eat from any tree of the garden'?" The woman said to the serpent, "From the fruit of the trees of the garden we may eat; but from the fruit of the tree which is in the middle of the garden, God has said, 'You shall not eat from it or touch it, or you will die.'" The serpent said to the woman, "You surely will not die! For God knows that in the day you eat from it your eyes will be opened, and you will be like God, knowing good and evil"* (Genesis 3:1-5).

Let's include GOD's original instruction to the male given on Sixth Day when he was created. There is an interesting variation between the original command and the words the woman used in her discussion with the serpent.

> *The LORD God commanded the man, saying, "From any tree of the garden you may eat freely; but from the tree of the knowledge of good and evil you shall not eat, for in the day that you eat from it you will surely die"* (Genesis 2:16-17).

In GOD's address to the man, He specifically said, *"from any tree of the garden you may eat freely,"* and then went on to qualify by specifying the one exception, the **tree of the knowledge of good and evil**. When the serpent addressed the woman, he immediately attacked GOD's statement of freedom. He did not say to the woman that GOD had forbidden eating from all the trees but his question to her made that **de facto** accusation. Technically, the question was not a charge against GOD. In fact, one could propose that the question was innocent and was born out of an unclear understanding of what GOD had said. That proposition is foolish, but the argument is the same type of statement as the question to begin with. You can almost hear the serpent defending himself by saying, "I didn't say that; it was just a question." Obviously, he could not use that defense with GOD. The point is that this illustrates how arguments that are deliberately ambiguous can become the basis for an offense against GOD. Often, in our rebellious moments, we concoct arguments of similar kind. We then defend our rebellion using similarly concocted defenses. It may be worthwhile to note that GOD is not fooled (mocked, Gal. 6:7) when we do such things, and they do not make us innocent of the offense.

In the same sense that permeated the implied accusation of the serpent against GOD, the woman now entered the conversation by attempting to clarify for the serpent what GOD had actually said. In fact, she repeats to the serpent what GOD actually did say by way of clarification. Inexplicably, though, she adds the phrase "or touch it" to her recitation. We said earlier that not touching the thing you were forbidden to eat would be a prudent course of action. But it was not in the command GOD had given to her husband. Perhaps her husband had instructed her incorrectly by adding that phrase. Or perhaps it was an understanding between the two of them designed to help them steer clear of the fruit. More likely, she simply added the seemingly innocent phrase in the moment. The "poison" in the serpent's tongue may have already begun its work in undermining her adherence to the command of GOD passed on to her by her husband. Each of these scenarios has its own quality, and any would contribute to the capacity of the serpent to deceive the woman when he spoke to her.

In any event, the woman clarified for the serpent that GOD had forbidden only the one fruit, not the fruit of all the trees. Her amplification of the command might be the first hint of the trouble soon to come. The subtle or crafty argument of the serpent drew her into his dialogue in such a way as to obscure the clarity, simplicity, and purity of GOD's command.[12] The serpent was on the offensive and the woman responded by going on the defensive rather than by ruling in the situation.[13] Once she became defensive, the serpent was able to use her defensiveness to drive home his key argument.

Now that the woman was engaging in the subtlety of the argument presented by the serpent, he could move to his direct accusation. The argument was that GOD was using the prohibition to withhold from the man and the woman something that was very valuable, or would be if they had access to it. He accused GOD of lying to the man and woman concerning the consequences of eating the fruit. GOD had said they would die.[14] The serpent then countered the Lord's words by declaring that eating the fruit would not result in their death.[15]

Essentially, the serpent accused GOD of withholding something important and good from them. If they ate the fruit, they would not die. On the contrary, the serpent argued, they would thenceforth "be like God" in that they would know "good from evil." He did not even present an argument as to how knowing good from evil would make them like GOD. Apparently, he felt that being like GOD would be important to them.[16] Having accused GOD of lying to the man and woman and having ascribed a false motivation to GOD, the serpent was finished with his task and things moved forward without any further involvement on his part. The woman had received the poison of his distorted argument and proceeded with her part of the implied bargain. By their joint reasoning, she would eat and not die, and in so doing would know good from evil, which would make her equivalent to GOD.[17] As we know, both her conclusions were wrong; knowing good from evil would not make her equivalent to GOD, and the death of her body did eventually come. More importantly, her status as a fully qualified son of GOD had been seriously compromised.

The Woman's Reasons

At this point, the woman commenced her inner conversation, so to speak. The serpent had driven a wedge between her and GOD through his declarations. That division having occurred, she proceeded to convince herself as to her course of action. She did not ask GOD or her husband in the matter. She decided for herself what she was going to do.

There were three things the woman noticed about the fruit as she considered the arguments and accusations the serpent had presented.

1. The fruit was pleasant in appearance.
2. The fruit appeared to be good food (pleasant to eat).
3. The fruit would make her wise (per the arguments of the serpent, not her own observation).

The first two ascriptions seem to be true at face value. In fact, the serpent said nothing about them. A thing is either pleasant to look at for any particular observer, or it is not. Something either looks like good food, or it doesn't. Whether it is good for food is independent of whether it looks like it is. But GOD had planted the tree in the garden Himself. There being no guile in GOD, we should assume that the fruit was good food if it looked like good food. There was no trap in the food. GOD was not being mean. The fruit was generally attractive and good to eat insofar as food is concerned. In fact, the fruit of *all the trees* in the garden were described in exactly that way before these events transpired (Gen. 2:9).

The third ascription needs closer analysis. What about the fruit made it appear to the woman to be capable of making her wise? Can we describe a relationship between visual appearance and an outcome like the opening up of wisdom? Even more important to us is the matter of whether knowing the difference between good and evil was (or is) actually wisdom. This observation seems to be the direct result of the dialogue with the serpent, not that a piece of fruit intrinsically looked capable of producing such a result.[18] However the woman arrived at the conclusion, once she had done so, believing the fruit would produce desirable wisdom in her, she acted on that conclusion. She ate the fruit.

Flesh of My Flesh

In the entire temptation narrative, the man was not mentioned. It's as though the conversation between the serpent and the woman took place in a context where they were alone. The text argues to the contrary, though. As soon as the woman ate the fruit she gave some of it to her husband who was "with her." The overwhelming implication is that the man was physically present during the conversation between his wife and the serpent. He was merely a spectator to the conversation, but he was there. We may wonder at his lack of participation. We may wonder why the serpent chose not to interact with him. We may wonder why the serpent did not interact with them both at the same time. All these musings aside, the serpent interacted with the woman while her husband remained present but mutely uninvolved.

Surely the man had a stake in the conversation and in its outcome. Whatever affected the woman would affect him. They were "one flesh," after all. Surely, in his mind, the two had the same things at stake here. But he seems to have simply stood by without being involved in any way until the woman presented him with fruit by way of inviting his participation. She had decided to accept the serpent's arguments and now was fully involving her husband in the results.

These observations beg the question, "Why did not the man intervene?" They were in full knowledge of GOD's prohibition concerning the fruit. But here the man was observing the conversation that had them eating the fruit in only a few moments. Could he not have prevented this outcome? Would his refusal have caused her to reevaluate her decision to eat? Even more importantly, why did he fail to come between the serpent and his wife to begin with?

We might argue that the exercise of vice-regal responsibility was the duty of only the man, or that he at least was designed to take the lead in such things. It was not the sole domain of the woman, in any event. The primary responsibility must have lain in the man. He should have been the target of the serpent's conversation but he was not. We may wonder why. Or perhaps he was the target in an indirect way.

It is difficult to avoid the conclusion that the man was responsible for his wife in ways in which she was not responsible for him.[19] He was, in some sense, responsible for the outcome of the conversation because he was responsible for his wife and her welfare. Conversely, she would not have been responsible for the outcome of the conversation had her husband been the target of the serpent because she was not responsible for his welfare, however interested she might be. She would likely share in the consequences of the decision, but would not in any way be responsible for those consequences.

So did the serpent fear to entangle the man in his arguments? Or was it a matter that the outcome was more certain with the woman? Could it be the fact that the man's responsibility might conflict with his desires and overcome the arguments of the serpent? The woman would have only her own desires to consider and might not have the countering influence of responsibility to sway her. We cannot know for certain how or why the serpent targeted the woman, but these considerations are likely factors.

Ultimately, however, the man clearly was responsible, as we shall see when we consider God's judgments.[20] I argue that the man knew as the events were underway that he was responsible for the outcomes. For that reason, it was in his (their) best interest to prevent the final outcome. He could have intervened at any point, even at the beginning of the conversation. He had the responsibility of a viceroy, which gave him dominion over the serpent.[21] After the conversation ended he could have prevented his wife from laying hold of the fruit. With his responsibility came the commensurate authority needed for any such intervention. There is no prior statement in scripture in which the man was specifically charged with this responsibility, but it is obvious this was the case, for both the husband and the viceroy. That being so, he must have known that he had that responsibility.

Nevertheless, the man did nothing to stop it. He too ate the fruit. Then they became "wise," "knowing good from evil." In becoming "wise" in this illegitimate manner, they also acquired a sense of shame, which manifested in a sudden awareness of their state of physical nakedness. Previously, this had not bothered them (Gen. 2:25 and 3:7 stand in contrast).

Aftermath

The viceroy had failed to adequately reflect the Father in The Creation. His broken relationship with his Father, in essence, now broke The Creation. Because the viceroy could not rule properly, that which he ruled lost the intended quality of his oversight. We shall soon see the impact of this in the pronouncements of God.

Before long, we will turn our attention to the dismissal of the viceroy from the garden that housed the tree of life and the intended "throne" of his rule. Before we do that, though, let's consider the transitional consequences of the disobedience of the man and woman. God did not take them to task immediately. Instead, He allowed them to experience the shame that grew out of their guilt, shame that became focused on their physical nakedness.[22] Their response to their guilt and shame was to hide from God.

It seems unlikely they were ashamed of their physical nakedness in the context of their own relationship to one another. The shame likely focused on the idea of nakedness in the presence of a third party, GOD, in this case. This shame-compensation took two forms. First, they made loin coverings (NASB) to compensate for what they now realized was physically uncovered. Then they took the strange step of attempting to hide entirely from GOD. They could not bear to be in His presence any longer in the state of physical nakedness or the newly felt spiritual nakedness. Conversely, He would know something was up if they were in His presence with their fig-leaf loin coverings. In a sense, they were trapped between two unacceptable alternatives, each of which was a form of exposure that they sought to avoid. They used the fig-leaf loin coverings to cover their physical nakedness and hid (presumably in the bushes) to "cover" their spiritual nakedness. So much for "wisdom."

It's not at all clear how long they thought they could hide from GOD. Eventually, they would need to be in His presence. [23] For now, they would remain hidden (or so they thought) until a better plan came along. Of course, they would soon find that the fig leaves they used for loin coverings would dry and become of no use to them. In both contexts, their hiding as a result of shame could only be temporary and would need regular renewal.[24] They would need to gather new fig-leaves regularly to fashion into loin coverings, and retire constantly to hiding places in order to avoid exposure. The man and woman had no real solution for the predicament occasioned by their newfound "knowledge" that had been presented to them as wisdom, so they panicked and used half-measures.

Into that setting, GOD introduced the first glimpse of His redemptive plan (after announcing His judgments). He gave to them animal skins to replace the fig-leaf coverings. In so doing, animals had to die and we get the very first shadow of blood sacrifice. As we know, this carries forward into the lives of Abel and Abraham and thence into the Levitical system. All of these things point to the final sacrifice of JESUS as described in Hebrews 10. The blood of the animals only pointed forward to the blood of GOD the Son in the person of JESUS the CHRIST.

The conversation between GOD and the man that occurred when GOD came looking for the now-covered and hiding couple is an interesting one. When the man explained his actions to GOD, he did not mention the infraction. He only mentioned his fear at GOD's coming and focused on the issue of his physical nakedness. The omniscient (all-knowing) GOD asked the rhetorical question, "Who told you that you were naked?" before confronting the man with the question regarding his infraction (Gen. 3:11). Of course, there was only one explanation and GOD knew what it was already. He just required the man to face up to the charges and his disobedient actions.

At that time there was no legal system in place. It appears that the man was required to understand the severity of his infraction by virtue of the awareness that had been placed in him by GOD at the time of his creation. There was no excuse he could make. He was simply guilty. However, he tried to shield himself by shifting the blame to the woman. In an instant, "Bone of my bones and flesh of my flesh" became "the woman you gave me" Because the woman was guilty as well, the focus shifted to her. In truly human dynamic, she immediately shifted the focus to the serpent.

GOD confronted the man with the question, "Where are you?" He confronted the woman with the question, "What is this you have done?" The verb that is translated "done" here might be better translated "made." In that case, GOD was confronting the woman with the fundamental change she had ushered into the earth.

The Judgments

All three of the actors seem to have been present at the time, or at least shortly thereafter. Why would the serpent be present at the time of GOD's interview of the man and woman? It seems likely that GOD summoned the serpent to the hearing or that a second hearing, to which the serpent was summoned, occurred soon thereafter. In either case, when the judgments were announced, the serpent was present.

First Judgment: (Serpent)

GOD pronounced the first judgment on the first actor in the temptation scenario, the tempter. He did not ask the serpent what he did or why. Neither did He question the veracity of the woman's report as to the serpent's involvement in the mischief regarding the fruit of the **tree of the knowledge of good and evil**. The serpent did what he did. We may posit that he was created to do what he did so that Man would have to choose to be a son of GOD, or a not-son. The serpent (as a manifestation of Satan) was not a son of GOD and could make no plea the Father would hear. Apparently, it was in the range of the serpent's nature to do what he had done. In fact, he apparently wasn't even expelled from the garden in the judgment GOD pronounced on him.

On the other hand, the serpent was not held guiltless. Retribution was meted out to him in the form of a permanent change in his being; he would become a crawling animal and be in perpetual enmity with the woman. Never again would he be able to exercise the same kind of influence over her. The curse did not physically separate Man and the serpent but it made for an always unpleasant relationship.[25]

One interesting aspect of the curse on the serpent is the announcement that the serpent would be wounded in his head by Man. At the same time, he would wound the heel of Man. This obviously metaphorical reference is quite revealing in that it provides a picture of relative power. A wounded (crushed) head is physiologically more serious than a bruised heel. This perpetual arrangement between Man and the serpent implies the eventual outcome of the struggle between Man and sin. Eventually and inevitably, the sons of GOD would overcome whatever impediments the metaphorical serpent (Satan according to Rev. 20:2) might place in their way.

Second Judgment: (Woman)

Having dispensed judgment on the serpent, GOD immediately moved on to address the woman. She had already confessed and there was no further discussion. GOD spoke to her concerning matters of reproduction, consigning her to endure difficulties in that aspect of her life. He also spoke to the nature of her relationship with her husband.[26] She had been brought forth as a suitable helper for the man. Now GOD made it clear that he would, in some sense at least, rule over her. This, as we know, set up the dynamic for the struggle between male and female that affects even the best of marriages. In a sense, the struggle is about power between the two. In this earliest of marriages, the competing goals of man and wife came into the earth.

It seems clear that these judgments were of a form that lasted from generation to generation. It was not just this one particular woman who would be so affected. The judgment was on the female human so long as marriage and reproductive phenomena should endure in the earth.

Third Judgment: (Man)

The viceroy was next. GOD immediately dealt with the responsibilities of the man. He phrased this judgment in a cause and effect format. The judgment on the man was a result of specific failure the man had exhibited in that he had complied with his wife's offer of sharing the fruit with him, knowing full well what GOD had said about it. To reiterate, it was his responsibility to protect her from the cunning of the serpent. It was also his responsibility to accurately represent GOD as His viceroy in the earth. He could fulfill neither of those responsibilities by eating the fruit, but he ate it anyway.

The scope of GOD's judgment on the man is staggering. The entire earth was affected. The ground itself was cursed. Specifically, it would now produce things that were harmful. It had been designed to produce plant life that, in turn, produced food for the living things on the earth, including Man. As a result of the curse it would now produce "thorns and thistles," which were contrary to the initial design and dynamic of the earth. It appears that thorns and thistles are a metaphor for the breaking of the harmony of the earth as it first came to be. Man would no longer be the viceroy of GOD. He would now be a creature who had to work hard in The Creation rather than properly ruling over it. The curse on the serpent indicates to us that Man would remain the primary creature in the earth, but his rule would now be much more difficult. Unlike the other living beings in the earth, Man would have to toil in order to eat. Some food would be as it had been and would continue to be for the other living creatures, but Man would have to labor hard to bring forth his necessary food, represented by bread in the pronouncement. Toiling stands in stark contrast to ruling, which had been the original intent and assignment for Man. Man could no longer take his life for granted. From this point on, more would be required of him than of any other creature.

Now came the clarification of human mortality. I have argued previously that Man is first a spiritual creature, and that his spirit, which is the core of his being, is "wrapped" in flesh, if you will. Certainly, the particular attention paid to the creation of Man implies the importance of the spirit in Man. The judgment of GOD regarding the man related to the flesh of the man (Gen. 3:19); it does not address his spiritual nature. Of course, it was the flesh that was involved in the infraction. The forbidden fruit enticed the woman as desirable food, and the eating of food is a phenomenon of the physical body and not of the spiritual person.

The flesh was thus condemned to a physical death in which dead dust was to return to dead dust after having been associated with living spirit. Had the man and woman rejected the arguments of the serpent as spiritual beings, this judgment would not have been necessary. Instead, they acted out of their souls for the gratification of the flesh and the human self. In their decision to act independently of the will of GOD their Father, they relegated the life-giving spirit to a secondary role. This is the most significant component of the need for redemption. Now they (and we) would need reconciliation with the Father, whose image and likeness in them (and us) had become so sullied.[27]

123

The Other Tree

We might wonder whether the man and woman ever ate fruit from the tree of life. The narrative suggests that they never did.[28] At the same time, we know that they were aware there was a **tree of life** and that they could have eaten its fruit. GOD placed the tree in the garden along with the **tree of the knowledge of good and evil**. He then instructed the man not to eat the fruit of the **tree of the knowledge of good and evil**. Apparently there were no instructions concerning the **tree of life**, one way or the other, except that it likely was included in their freedom to eat "from any tree in the garden" (Gen. 2:16). It was there, but the dialogue between the serpent and the woman does not mention that tree at all.

On the other hand, the real issue was that they ate from the **tree of the knowledge of good and evil**. Perhaps they had eaten from the tree of life previously. In that case, the demarcation was the fall. It might be that before the two ate the fruit from the **tree of the knowledge of good and evil**, they had eaten regularly from the tree of life. Having once fallen, though, they could no longer be permitted to eat from that tree, as we shall see.

At the time GOD issues His judgments, however, the **tree of life** again attracts attention. Having announced that Man was now subject to death of the physical body, He states that the man should be separated from the **tree of life**. This was to be accomplished by permanently expelling the man and his wife from the garden, thus cutting off their access to the **tree of life**. The Lord guaranteed they could not return by assigning angels to guard the entrance to the garden.[29]

Would eating the fruit of the **tree of life** have "cancelled" the judgment of GOD once it had been announced? That is unlikely. GOD is never arbitrary, and having announced physical death for the man, it is unlikely that any phenomenon could have set that judgment aside.[30] Perhaps the announcement of GOD was a formal one that accompanied the expulsion. Another possibility is that GOD was looking at the future generations of the man and woman who might not eat the wrong fruit (knowledge of good and evil) and eat the fruit of the **tree of life** and produce a very complex dynamic for mankind in our relationships with God. Most likely, the failure of the viceroy set the condition of that failure in the human soul in perpetuity, insofar as the efforts of Man are concerned. The failure of the one would mark the spiritual history of the whole.[31]

Without His saying so, these events set into motion *the dynamics of redemption.* The failure of the first viceroy disqualified all his future generations from the full exercise of his vice-regnal status. The condition of that disqualification would remain in the human soul in perpetuity unless God Himself provided a solution.[32] But He would come who would overcome the disqualification when He came as a man to provide the mechanism for the reinstatement of Man.[33] [34] In some sense, then, the **tree of life** became a non-issue for the ordinary history of man. Only in the millennial age does the tree appear again with its eternal functions (Rev. 22:1-2). The **tree of the knowledge of good and evil**, by the way, becomes irrelevant and passes out of existence, so far as we know.

Eve

Adam named Eve as his last act in the context of the garden in which he was the viceroy. It is not clear that he did so because he had been assigned to name things or because the separation the fruit had made between them required it to be so. Perhaps they had not needed a name for her before that point. It is not likely that any inquiry as to why she now needed a name could produce a fully reliable answer, but as they left the garden he began to call her Eve (Hebrew c*h*ava), which means "life."

While the name of the man was not used in the text until Genesis 2:20, it appears from subsequent text that it was God who gave the name Adam to the man (Gen. 5:2).[35] So God named Adam, Adam called the woman that was taken from him "woman," and then Adam named her Eve as they were leaving the garden in Eden.

The naming of the woman at this point emphasizes the separateness of the man and woman from that time. It is likely that there was no competition between them prior to the consumption of the forbidden fruit. At some level, sin is a manifestation of self-centeredness. Perhaps before the failure, the man and woman had been able to co-exist in a much more cooperative way.

Some Other Considerations

It is a characteristic of this book and others I have written to pursue the central topic through the lens of scripture and not other fields of inquiry. As a result of this deliberate approach to the work, and the more-or-less thematic approach I have taken, scripture itself places limitations on me.

The Eden narrative, particularly the fall, is packed with meaning on a large number of dimensions. It was not possible to cover every possible question in this analysis. For many, the early chapters of the book of Genesis are mostly allegorical. In this treatment I have taken them to be *literal* (at least in intent) however *obscure* the material may be. When one approaches such narratives from a literal perspective, there is no way to fully cover every possible idea that might be presented because the allegorist looks perpetually for new meanings. With more obscure materials, the effort to find new meaning will be limitless. Unfamiliarity of the context of the material adds to the need some feel to find new lines of interpretation. That is not a bad thing per se, but it sometimes contributes to disagreement with even the most straightforward interpretations.

The early narrative material of Genesis is also *cryptic* (brief) in its nature. The scope of the events and their eternal linkages and consequences are often stated in the most cursory manner. There is just so much more that could have been recorded but was not, given the practical concerns of scripture. Much is simply left to us wrapped in mystery. It is not unhealthy or unwise to peer into the mysteries of scripture (Heb. 2). We are even encouraged to do so and this is a time in the providences of GOD when such peering may well be rewarded with revelation. "If any of you lacks wisdom let him ask of God" (Ja. 1:5). This is an instruction of scripture itself. Of course, the inquiry must be honest. We must be careful lest we use scripture to support unscriptural doctrines.

Finally, the actual, strange *physical context* in which the matters discussed so far took place cannot safely be deemed to be the same as those currently in place. There are clear hints in the text that this is so. As we proceed in this analysis, we likely will be challenged to release our points of view in many aspects of the sacred history. As we have already seen, some matters just won't fit into our preconceptions. What we have believed has been so heavily influenced by education and doctrine as to make the straightforward interpretation of this section of scripture practically unrecognizable to us. In an earlier chapter, I attempted to help us recognize that some aspects of the scientific method make it very difficult to accept what scripture says. It is not the purpose of this work, though, to attempt to bring harmony between the knowledge of science, which is GOD-excluding, and scripture, which is GOD-oriented. That work is for other analyses than this one.

These three aspects of early sacred history (obscurity, brevity, and strangeness) should not frustrate us. We should face them squarely, with the full understanding that GOD has given us enough to enable us to grasp important matters and patterns in them. The dual themes of sonship and redemption have directed the analysis and will continue to do so. Our attempt is to find and understand the beginnings of these themes in holy writ. Other matters have not been so important. This has resulted in some common themes of religious inquiry being relatively neglected herein. This does not make those matters unimportant, but the focus of this work is just different.

There are many questions that people raise about non-central issues in this early material. Most of those questions are more curiosity than anything else. Some of these we have touched on, some not. It is simply beyond the scope of this book to peer into all those questions. Often, the answers do not contribute very much to our spiritual understanding anyway. Some are

127

mere distractions. I ask the readers to pursue such things if they wish, but I will not spend the time to complete those analyses in this work.

Recapitulation

It seems worthwhile to provide a brief summary of our analysis up to this point. The exclusion from Eden's garden was such a turning point that most things of interest to us simply changed after that. After we review, we will move forward to the next major turning point: the flood. These are not really turning points. GOD never got off narrative. Human beings, though, brought about conditions that resulted in very drastic changes in the story of GOD and His love for sons.

We begin with the fact that one of the major characteristics of GOD is that He loves. Scripture even makes the declaration, "God is love" (1 Jn. 4:16). Before there was a creation, GOD existed in a context we call "the Godhead." In that context, GOD the Father and GOD the Son enjoyed a relationship characterized as much by love as by anything else. The Father and the Son determined that they would share that relationship with other beings. There being no other beings with whom this sharing could occur they determined to bring such beings into existence. Because these beings were to be created, it was necessary to produce a creation into which to place them. The Creation came about as a result of the Father and the Son needing a context for other sons. Scripture begins by describing the acts of creation. Interestingly, those acts follow for the most part a sequence that aligns fairly well with what science has designated as the proper order of events.

Not only did GOD determine to love His apex creature, He also decided to make that creature into something that had the capacity to represent GOD inside The Creation. GOD could not inhabit The Creation, as it actually resides in Him. But He could have a "perfect" representative of Himself inside The Creation to rule it as He would rule it. This "son" was also to be a viceroy for his Father.

GOD created a very particular location from which the new son would exercise his dominion as viceroy. Into that particular location, GOD also placed two very special trees with the purpose of providing the viceroy the opportunity to rule or to be ruled. If the viceroy could not choose to exercise dominion, he could not accurately or adequately represent his Father, GOD, in The Creation.

Having completed these works of creation, GOD rested. His new son then began his rule as viceroy in the earth. He began by naming animals as GOD sent them to him. Then GOD brought to "birth" the woman who had been created hidden in the man. Very shortly thereafter, the woman was approached by the serpent in his effort to seduce her soul away from GOD. By persuading the woman of his arguments, the serpent was able to influence both the woman and the man to surrender the authority of viceroy. When they did that, they elevated their souls above their spirits and lost much of the character of GOD that had been entrusted to them.

These things having happened, GOD had no choice except to remove the man from his position as ruler in the earth. This, in turn, meant he had to be removed from the garden (the holy of holies). Furthermore, GOD also permitted disorder to enter the world as He no longer had an adequate viceroy. These actions set into motion the mechanism of redemption.

---

[1] They were not of the substance of The Eternal *per se*, being created, and were less than it, but had as of yet nothing in them that could discredit them. GOD knew, of course, that they would fail, but they did not have to. Insofar as The Creation was concerned, however, they were perfect.

[2] We sometimes have a hard time understanding how GOD could know they would fail and yet His knowledge was not the cause of the fall. The cause of the fall was not GOD's knowledge of it. The cause was that the man and woman succumbed to the desire to be equal with GOD. Philippians 2:6 reveals that JESUS did not seek such a thing even though He could have. The cause of the fall was not GOD's knowledge; it was their contempt for His primacy.

[3] It makes perfect sense that the ultimate creature would be the last creature. In a way, the process of creation was a kind of crescendo culminating in the introduction of the viceroy.

[4] It seems reasonable to suppose there was only one continent at that time. Eden was at least east of center of that continent. It was not completely at the east end of the continent because Cain later was exiled in that direction. East is an important direction as far as GOD is concerned. This is reflected in the fact that Judah (the tribe which kept the scepter in trust) was always camped in the east during the desert sojourn. In any event, GOD planted the "holy place" (Eden) in the east.

[5] I have argued before that the creation has a kind of "consciousness." Minimally, it responds to GOD and to the sons of GOD, as in Romans 8. Even the stones would have cried out at the coming of JESUS to the time and place of His glorification (Lk. 19:40).

[6] GOD made it especially, so it is holy. He created the entire continent, but He did nothing special to it. When He created Eden on the continent, it became a focal point, so it fits the model of a holy place as shown to Moses on the mountain (Ex. 25:40; Acts 7:44). Then He turned His attention further to a special garden in the special region. It was a holy place within a holy place. It was a holy of holies.

[7] In its center, GOD placed two trees not otherwise found in the earth, not even in Eden outside the garden. Revelation 22:1-5 contains a narrative related to the **tree of life**. It seems the **tree of the knowledge of good and evil** has passed away for good.

[8] This argues for a very early unfolding of the narrative of the fall in Eden (Gen. 3:22). Had they eaten from the **tree of life** first, they might not have eaten of the other fruit. We simply don't know. Alternatively, we might suppose that they could have eaten from the **tree of life** but that the instance of sin changed their potentials. After that, then, in this scenario, they had to be forbidden access to the **tree of life**. It was not access to the **tree of the knowledge of good and evil** that mattered any longer.

[9] Revelation 12:9 equates the serpent, the dragon, and Satan. It was a long road from inducing a woman to eat some fruit to ruling the great false prophet at the end of the age. It's like the serpent grew up to be one who will seek to rule the earth instead of the sons of GOD.

[10] The serpent "spoke" to the woman. Did all animals speak before the fall? This seems to be another very unusual case. The text is obviously speaking of Satan, or so we suppose. After the tree incident, it appears to be the case that the usefulness of the snake was ended, but Satan's relationship with the serpent seems to persist. Perhaps Satan took on the guise of a serpent. If so, then GOD would not have cursed the serpent but Satan himself. Some things to think about.

[11] At the most crucial time in the life of JESUS, He said, "not my will, but Yours be done" (Lk. 22:42). This stands in stark contrast to the response of Adam and Eve when it was suggested they could be like GOD in the face of His command.

[12] Sophistication of argument, while it may be academically attractive, might also be a sign of the weakness or irrelevance of an argument. Perhaps she was even trying to impress the serpent.

[13] Perhaps the woman was also rejecting the authority of her husband in the moment (1 Cor. 11:10), which made her susceptible to the arguments of the serpent.

[14] Genesis 2:17 uses the Hebrew term *mot tamut* in this instance. Its literal meaning is something like, "dying you will die," which is interpreted in a variety of ways, the most compelling of which is, "you will certainly begin to die."

[15] Note that physical death did not immediately follow eating the fruit; however, Man became mortal and therefore subject to death. One may argue that the loss of the position of viceroy was equivalent to death. In any event, the serpent did not use the word death in the same way GOD used it originally. It was his way to twist the plain meaning of that which GOD had decreed.

[16] Genesis 3:22 reveals that GOD saw the matter differently. GOD announced that the result was the risk of eternal life in Man's now broken state. However, before eternal life could now be granted, redemption of fallen Man was needed.

[17] Her determination stands in interesting contrast to the determination of JESUS found in Philippians 2:6.

[18] First John 2:15-17 provides us with a different point of view in the matter; lust of the eyes (appearance), lust of the flesh (food-worthiness), and pride of life (making one wise) are presented as three dimensions of "love of the world." This also evoked the three temptations of JESUS in the wilderness, as found in Matthew 4.

[19] To the man had been given responsibility for the welfare of the woman. While she was equally yoked to him, her responsibilities were not the same as his. She was not responsible for his welfare in the situation. He had the responsibility to cover her head, but not she, his (1 Cor. 11:5-10).

[20] The woman's judgment related to child bearing, while the man's was the breaking of The Creation, according to Genesis 3:17-19.

[21] Perhaps the serpent pursued the woman because he was actually subject to the rule of the man while she was not. In that scenario, he could not go up against the man as the man had the investiture of a measure of divine authority.

[22] They became aware of their physical nakedness, not of what had caused it, per se. Hence, they sought to cover what they thought was the problem. In fact, there was nothing to be done to compensate for the actual sin. The emphasis on their physical nakedness was all they could do. Their souls had separated them from GOD and the resulting obscuration of their actual identities caused them to focus on their flesh. In a sense, their obscured souls made it impossible for them to "look up" to the heavens.

[23] Was the meeting in the cool of the day customary, or was this the only time? The text does not state the case one way or another. We often assume this was something they did regularly. If so, it was really a blessed state to be in. If it was only the first time that GOD showed up at that time of day, imagine the wretchedness they must have felt when He did show up and they had to remain hidden (as they thought).

[24] The writer of Hebrews makes it clear in chapters 9 and 10 that all efforts of men that point at redemption, even those sanctioned and prescribed by GOD, need repetition. Only redemption provided by GOD is effective on a perpetual basis.

[25] The bruising of the heel has a specific application in the relationship between Satan and JESUS. It has a more general application to his ongoing harassment of humans. Interestingly, GOD told Isaiah that even after predation was removed from the earth, the curse would remain on the serpent. His subjection to the man would involve the bruising of his head in perpetuity.

[26] One way of reading Genesis 3:16 is to conclude that the woman would be perpetually needful of a relationship with the man. Out of that need, she would be susceptible to his rule. Another way to read the passage is to compare it to the one other passage of similar kind in Genesis 4:7 where GOD warns Cain to not let sin master him through its "desire" for him. One may conclude from this comparison that GOD was telling the woman that she would desire to dominate her husband but that it wouldn't work out well and he would dominate her instead. This seems to be the root of the often political nature of most marriages, in which the couple negotiate for power rather than seek harmonious cooperation.

[27] This reminds us of Esau's bowl of soup. He, in effect, scorned his inheritance for a very small exchange (Gen. 25:27-34). Adam and Eve risked virtually everything in their contempt for the primacy of GOD.

[28] This argues that the events in Genesis 3 took place in a very short period of time, perhaps only days. However, it may be that they did eat from the **tree of life** before they became flawed. Perhaps the fall more or less cancelled their previous use of the **tree of life**. After the eating of the other fruit, though, the whole thing changed and they somehow lost the life they had gained. Then it was necessary to disallow their further access to the **tree of life**.

[29] Esau could not regain his inheritance despite his bitter search for reinstatement (Heb. 12:15-17). Adam and Eve were prevented perpetually from regaining access to the tree of life (Gen. 3:22-24). It is not likely that the garden in Eden survived the flood in Noah's time.

[30] It appears that physical death is used as a metaphor for eternal judgment. These things do not appear to be negotiable.

[31] *"As in Adam all die, so also in Christ all will be made alive"* (1 Cor. 15:20-22). This passage makes clear the necessity for divine redemption, rather than the tears and efforts of man.

[32] "*All of us like sheep have gone astray…but the Lord has caused the iniquity of us all to fall on Him*" (Is. 53:6).

[33] First Corinthians 15:20-22 makes it clear that there is only One who can get this done. Life was lost in Eden. It was recovered in CHRIST.

[34] This analysis presents a particular point of view that may be regarded as being at variance with most others. My purpose is to round out what we know through consideration of a new perspective.

[35] Adam as a man was a specific category of creation: Man. In this book I use Man for the category, man for any exemplar of Man, and Adam as the proper name of the first man.

CHAPTER SEVEN

HUMANITY IN EXILE

Irrevocable judgment had been pronounced, forcing the man and woman to leave the garden (which was a type of the "holy of holies") that GOD had planted in Eden (which was a type of the "holy place"). At the same time, the earth had become subject to all kinds of woes. GOD had said to Adam, "*Cursed is the ground because of you*" (Gen. 3:17). The ground surely lost some of the quality GOD had built into it at the beginning. A curse on the ground would undo some of its blessedness, so to speak, and that loss of quality would begin to cause negative things to occur in and to the earth. These things would happen in the earth itself and also in the plant life it produced.[1] As the man and woman (Adam and Eve) left the garden in Eden, the earth was already beginning to become less than it had been. Soon, thorns and brambles would come from what had been blessed ground.

It appears that the loss of the "blessedness" of the ground was not apparent all at once. For example, in a later chapter we will discuss the Noahic flood as an event of tremendous impact on the earth. The earth before the flood and the earth after the flood were significantly different and impacted all life in important ways. Perhaps the greatest changes took place as a result of the flood, even though they were set into motion in the garden in Eden.

Adam and Eve had been sentenced to permanent exile. In fact, they are typological for the human condition from that time. In other

133

words, they brought exile to all humanity in perpetuity. Not only could they not return to the garden in Eden, GOD made certain that it was impossible for any human ever to find the garden again. This adds fuel to the argument of the allegorists. Since we can't find Eden, they say, it must only be an idea from some utopian view of humanity. That is not what the Bible says, though. The text apparently is intended to be taken literally, however typological its elements may be.

We know very little about Adam after the exile. In essence, we know only that he had sons (and daughters, Gen. 5:4) after his eviction, but that is about all. It is easy to imagine times of bitter regret over the matter of the fruit of the **tree of the knowledge of good and evil**. The disappointment of Adam's removal from his position as viceroy of GOD in the garden in Eden resulted in a whole new life for him, a life of toil. This was not the life that was intended for the son of GOD at the time of his creation. GOD intended for him to rule a harmonious world, but instead he introduced disharmony.[2] Adam knew well the distinction between what was intended and what resulted from his non-decision concerning the fruit. Nonetheless, he lived a very long life with that reality always present in his mind.

Genesis 3:23 does not specify that the exile caused Adam and Eve to leave the area of Eden, only its garden. It is almost certainly the case that they remained in Eden, but were unable to return to the garden area. The figurative "holy of holies" remained off limits (even hidden) to them, but the "holy place" of Eden was their home.[3] Even so, Adam had to toil continually for his provision.

Cain and Abel

The Bible does not say that Cain was the first son (or child) of Adam and Eve. It only says Eve so named him. There is a strong implication that he was at least the firstborn son of the pair (daughters are not specified in the listings).[4] Likewise, the text does not specify that Abel was the second son of Adam and Eve, only that he was younger than Cain. Furthermore, by the time Abel was born, there might have been many sons and daughters in Adam's family. Cain and Abel are highlighted in the early part of Genesis 4 because they are the two persons about whom the story is told.

It is hard to imagine that Adam and Eve did not share the story of their woes with their children. Cain and Abel must have known of the events of that fateful day in the garden and of the things that occurred afterward. They would have known, for example, that GOD preferred the skin of an animal as a loin covering over vegetable material such as fig leaves. Surely they would have informed their children of the consequences they suffered when they ate the fruit. Such things were central stuff of the family ethos. Both Cain and Abel would have that family wisdom from the time they could understand such things. They were not alone in the world, and to the extent we can understand such things, there can be little doubt this was part of their culture. We cannot know what wisdom Adam and Eve extracted from their early experiences, nor how they interpreted the exile when explaining it to their sons. It is not likely that they claimed that GOD was picking on them because both sons in this narrative did offer sacrifices to GOD and Cain even had a subsequent dialogue with GOD.

Somehow the two sons, Cain and Abel, knew things that led them to offer sacrifices to GOD (Genesis 4:3-4). They knew to make the sacrifices from the produce of their economic activities (not monetary but useful to their families). One wonders whether Adam and Eve also offered sacrifices after their expulsion from the garden.[5] It seems likely that Adam was the one who taught his sons to perform sacrifices from the fruit of their labors.

Both farming and herding animals are useful forms of work. Each of them has been necessary since the expulsion from the garden (Gen. 3:19). Why Cain was a farmer and Abel was a herdsman is not hinted at in the passage; those were just the paths they followed. Perhaps Adam assigned their duties as a division of labor. There is no reason to think one was more useful than the other. It is not that animals were more important. In fact, we do not have any information that the animals were used for food (Gen. 1:29-30). Perhaps the animals were useful only in terms of clothing, milk, and cheese. We simply do not know.[6]

However things came to be, each of the two sons had a trade, as we say. Each of them knew to offer sacrifices to GOD, and that the sacrifices should come from their respective trades.[7] These conditions form the backdrop for the story of Cain and Abel. The text tells us that on a certain occasion Cain offered sacrifices from the crops his labor as a farmer had produced. There is no mention that these were the firstfruits. Conversely, there is no suggestion that Cain was stingy or anything else. At about the same time (possibly somewhat later) Abel also offered sacrifices from the animals he had under his care. In Abel's case, though, he offered firstborn animals and their fat portions, pre-figuring Levitical observances.[8]

The text does not reveal how Abel knew the right things to do. As I mentioned before, it is not unreasonable to assume that the two sons lived in Eden, although outside the garden. The exile had involved the garden, and Adam and Eve almost certainly remained in Eden and raised their sons there. This was a "particular" land in that GOD had given it special care. In a sense, then, Eden likely was unlike any place we know in the earth today. It was still blessed by the special touch of GOD. It is also possible that Adam and Eve were much more immediately conversant with GOD than we are now. Perhaps (probably) Cain and Abel were also still quite conversant with Him. The conversation between Cain and GOD, for example, certainly implies this.

Furthermore, we have no information as to why GOD "had regard" for Abel's sacrifice but not for Cain's. That He did show preference is clear, but we do not know why He did so. It is to this fact that the text draws our attention. As would be true for you and me, Cain was offended that GOD preferred his brother's sacrifice but showed "no regard" for his own. GOD, knowing full well what was going on in Cain's heart, asked him to explain his reaction (rhetorically) and went on to explain that a proper sacrifice would get a different result. The Lord went on to say that improper conduct would lead to domination by sin, but that Cain needed to master sin. This is an important matter. We must master sin or it will master us. Such is the universal plight of fallen humanity. The responsibility for mastering sin, GOD said, lay in Cain himself, as in us. Sin desires to master us, but we must master sin. There is no third option.

Cain, having received these admonitions from GOD, nevertheless permitted sin to overtake him. The sacrifice he had offered was not a sin; it just did not meet the Lord's standard. Now sin mastered Cain, and he murdered his brother. It is doubtful he thought this would change GOD's mind. More likely, it was a matter of revenge born in jealousy. Abel had offered a suitable sacrifice and GOD had shown approval. Apparently, Cain wanted GOD's approval as well and was angered when he didn't get it. He might have repented and brought to GOD another more acceptable sacrifice. Instead, he took out his anger on his brother, who had done him no harm. Had Abel not offered an acceptable sacrifice, Cain's still would not have been acceptable. The two sacrifices were independent of one another. GOD wasn't worried about first place in the matter. His concern was for the hearts of the two brothers.

But Cain allowed his jealousy to turn into a murderous rage against his brother Abel, and he employed a subterfuge. One reading suggests that Cain told Abel about his disappointment, while another says that Cain invited Abel into the field and there simply killed him. These differences have to do with the construction of the Hebrew phrases. An alternate translation might be, "and Cain told his brother *while* they were in the field and killed him there." The word "while" is not present in the Hebrew text and so, arguably, this is not a correct translation. However it happened, Cain took opportunity to kill his brother when they were away from the rest of the family.

A notable feature of this narrative is that Adam and Eve are not present in the portrayed events. One wonders whether Adam's presence would have helped moderate Cain's rage. Had Adam been present, Cain might at least have delayed in carrying out his purpose, and perhaps his ardor would have cooled. It might be that Adam is not present in the narrative just to convey to us the importance of fathers in our lives. Alas, Cain did not alter his purpose, and he murdered his brother.[9]

Cain's actions brought about four notable results. First, by killing his brother, he eliminated all his brother's future generations from the earth. Murdering one person is like murdering an entire people. Second, Abel's words are lost to us. Obviously, Abel was a righteous man.[10] His words might have been instructive for us. Murdering one person is paramount to eliminating his wisdom from the world. Third, it demonstrated the verity of GOD's warning about mastering sin. Finally, the murder of Abel caused Cain to experience exile beyond the borders of Eden. He could no longer be found in the blessed land.[11] Cain's exile would take him away from his parents and any siblings he had at the time. After he went into that exile, he would build a race that was based culturally on his own unrighteousness.

"Where is Abel Your Brother?"

The fateful question came. Surely Cain was aware that GOD would know of the death of his brother and its manner. In the heat of his anger, he might not have had that conscious thought, but after the murder, it surely must have occurred to him. In fact, he might have selected the field as the location for his murder in an attempt to avoid detection. That is unknown. In any event, upon his next encounter with GOD, this was the question GOD led off with.

As we so often do, Cain attempted to avoid the question. In this case, there was no one else to blame as Adam had shifted the focus to Eve, and Eve to the serpent in the matter of the fruit of the **tree of the knowledge of good and evil**. In a sense, though, Cain did attempt to shift the focus. In essence, he blamed Abel himself. It is as though he said, "Abel is a grown man and does what he wants. Who am I to keep up with him or tell him what to do?" Of course, GOD's question was not about that. His question was designed to bring forth the truth so that Cain would confront that truth before judgment came.

Cain's response, like his earlier sacrifice, was inadequate. GOD, full knowing the truth of Abel's death, and hearing Cain's evasive and somewhat angry response, spoke directly to the matter. Abel's righteous blood called to GOD from the ground. In some sense, GOD was testifying that The Creation was sensitive to what had happened. He was also testifying that righteousness mattered to Him.

Doubled Curse

At the time He judged Adam and Eve in the matter of the fruit of the **tree of the knowledge of good and evil**, GOD cursed the ground because of Adam's failure. In the case of the murder of Abel, GOD now cursed Cain from the ground. For Adam, toil would be required and he would have to cultivate the ground rather than simply having food made available to him. For Cain, even toil would not be very successful. Because he had caused his brother's blood to be spilled on the ground, it (the ground) would not "yield its strength" to him. As a result, he would be largely unsuccessful and virtually homeless. The Creation would not welcome him and be subject to his efforts. He had been a farmer, but now farming would not work well for him. The text goes on to say that wandering (in search of sustenance?) would be part of his lot. He was "cursed from the ground."

Let's be clear. GOD cursed the ground because of Adam's sin. Only great toil would cause the ground to yield, when before it had yielded food readily. Now the same ground would fail to yield specifically even to the toil that Cain might pour out on it. Rather than yield food, the ground now kept the blood of Abel insofar as Cain was concerned. The Creation itself had become a testimony both to Cain's evil and Abel's righteousness.

Cain's reaction to GOD's judgment was immediate and strong. He immediately felt fear concerning his future and expressed that his curse was out of bounds. Everything he had ever known was taken from him. He would even lose his relationship with GOD. The most cogent aspect of his reaction was his fear that he would simply be killed out of hand by anyone who encountered him.

Perhaps GOD wanted Cain to serve as a reminder in the earth of the consequences of fratricide. Had He desired to punish Cain with death beyond the punishment He had meted out to Adam regarding mortality, He could simply have caused Cain to die immediately. He did not do so. Cain expressed the fear that came out of his guilt. The memory of Cain's heinous crime would remain in the earth as long as Cain remained.

GOD's reaction to Cain's fear of death was to mark him in some manner. The mark would carry with it an implicit warning to anyone who encountered him, to prevent their killing him offhand. Much speculation has been devoted to the nature of the mark of Cain.[12] Cain's survival was important to Cain; the reminder of what Cain had done was important to GOD.

Another Culture

One result of Cain's wandering exile was his removal from the culture of his father Adam. Adam's culture retained, no doubt, not only the memory of the garden but also the memory of his exile from the garden. He would also have remembered and passed on to his children the memory of walking with GOD in the cool of the day. He would have remembered that he had ruled the world for a brief time. He would have remembered an unbroken creation, one in which food was readily available with no toil. He would have remembered a time when there was no shame, and no awareness of the difference between good and evil. However he felt about these things, he would have remembered them and preserved their memory through what he taught his children. These were the components of Adam's culture. It is likely, or at least quite possible, that Adam also was entrusted with the saga of creation, to put that knowledge into the earth and keep it alive.

Cain had not known the garden; only his father's stories. He did not remember a time of no toil. Shame had become an inseparable part of the human soul. The earth was already broken before he was born.[13] While he would have remembered what his father had told him, he would have known most of it only in a second-hand way. Now he was sundered, in effect, from everything his father had taught him, and his new and very different life led him to develop a worldview quite different from that of his father Adam. Inevitably, Cain began a new culture of his own that also was quite different from that of Adam, Eve, and their sons who remained with them in Eden. In other words, Cain started over with no real connection to his earlier life. Initially, we can't even be sure he had children.[14] In any event, as Cain began this life of exile, he would be its prominent character and would mark it very strongly with his own history rather than that of his father.

There were now two cultures in the world. One of them was characterized by a fairly accurate sense of GOD and His ways. The other culture, Cain's, was not so accurate in that regard. The two cultures were estranged for the most part. Enmity inevitably marked the early years of their awareness of one another; Cain out of his fear of retribution, and Adam's other descendants out of the memory of the murder.[15] They would, at least for a while, be separated geographically. Furthermore, there was likely a physical distinction (Cain's mark) that separated them from one another in appearance.

In a sense, we may tentatively suggest there were two ethnicities in the world. Realizing the sensitivity that is associated with the word, I will use the term "Race of Cain" to refer to him and his descendants.[16] At the same time, I will use the term "Race of Seth" to refer to the other main group. These two "races" would co-exist in the world, but for some time there would not be very much contact between them. Eventually, though, Seth's descendants may have needed to move out of Eden and into parts of the world inhabited by Cain's descendants. By that time, however, the two "peoples" were significantly different in their worldviews.

Cain's "Race"

Scripture doesn't say much about Cain's descendants. Several of them are listed along with certain things they did, but Cain's race is not central to the purposes of GOD. Cain did have descendants after he left the locale in which his parents lived, presumably Eden.

Interestingly, although Cain was "cursed from the land" and was doomed to be a wanderer, he founded a city after his son Enoch was born. It is likely this was a small place and was established as much for defense as for commerce, because Cain was so driven by fear and paranoia. Several other generations receive mention only in passing until the text comes to a fellow named Lamech. This fellow, having two wives, provides us with the first recorded instance in scripture of polygamy. In Lamech we see the *perpetuation of violence* in the murder of a young man against whom he had a grievance, and of a second man as well. He had worked out somehow that there would be no punishment for his murder. By Lamech's time, guilt might well have become an obsolete idea in Cain's culture.

The Early Generations of Cain

- Cain
- Enoch (<u>not</u> the same Enoch born to Jared in the line of Seth)
- Irad
- Mehujael
- Methushael
- Lamech (*not* the Lamech who was the father of Noah in the line of Seth)
- Adah (wife of Lamech)
- Jabal (pastoral—son of Lamech and Adah)
- Jubal (musician—son of Lamech and Adah)
- Zillah (wife of Lamech)
- Tubal-cain (metallurgist—son of Lamech and Zillah))
- Naamah (daughter of Lamech and Zillah)

Lamech's sons are noted in scripture in association with some of their impacts on the culture:

- Jabal was noted for his pastoral life
- Jubal was noted for his love of musical instrumentation
- Tubal-Cain was noted for his skill as a metallurgist

This short genealogical treatment gives us virtually no other information. It is as though Cain's race passed out of memory except for the fact that some of the descendants of Seth married some of the women who were descendants of Cain. As we shall see, this caused some problems, not the least of which was an earth-changing flood.

Seth's "Race"

Adam's descendants have now separated into two major groups. Cain seems to have gone into exile before Seth was born. So Seth was born into a family that had the memory of Cain and Abel, but he himself did not know them. Genesis 4:25 makes it very clear that his birth was after the exile.

Of the two sons, Cain and Abel, Abel seems to have better identified with his parents and their worldview. This suggests to us that, even though Adam and Eve were under an exile judgment, they still retained the knowledge of GOD. When Seth was born, his mother testified to her hope that Seth would take after his older brother Abel with regards to adhering to their culture. Nothing in scripture suggests this was not the case.

While Cain's progeny receive brief and cursory treatment in scripture and then drop out of the story, the "race" of Seth continues to appear prominently throughout the biblical record. In fact, it is Seth's bloodline that eventually produced JESUS (Lk. 3:23-38). It is in this race that the memory of GOD was best preserved. By the way, Noah also was of the race of Seth.

Scripture notes Seth's birth in a very interesting way. Just as it says that Man was made in the "image and likeness" of GOD, it also says that Seth was born in the image and likeness of his father Adam (Gen.

5:3). These things matter. Furthermore, Seth came forth as a replacement for his older brother Abel, whom Cain had murdered. This hints at substitutionary phenomena which would enter scripture in many forms later. All such forms point to the substitutionary aspects of the work of JESUS the CHRIST.

We cannot with certainty say that Seth was exactly son number three to Adam and Eve. In fact, Adam was 130 years old when Seth was born. What we need to know is that the bloodline was reckoned through Seth. I propose that this is because *Seth was most like his father Adam in preserving the culture given by GOD to Adam.* He was the best representation of Adam, and therefore of GOD, among the sons of Adam. In some sense, he was the image and likeness of his father Adam. The rest of chapter 5 of Genesis delineates the line of Seth down to the time of Noah. For each generation, the man named was the key representative in that generation. In other words, what was preserved for us is the name of that man who was most GOD-like among his brothers. For none of those generations do we know the number of sons or the birth order of the key individual. In each generation, the man named kept the faith alive, so to speak. The others made sons and daughters to inhabit the earth.

So Seth was born third or later to Adam and Eve. Given Adam's age at the time of Seth's birth, Seth might have been son number ten or twenty or whatever. To us it matters he was the keeper of the faith.[17] The "Race of Seth" is a term by which I mean the whole set of Seth's progeny. At the same time, the particular bloodline leading to the Redeemer is the line of the "priests of the world," so to speak. GOD noted their spiritual stature and relied on them to pass on the knowledge of Him.

We do not know how many sons or grandsons Seth had. We just know that Enosh was not the only one. Seth also had daughters, none of whom are mentioned by name. Again, we do not know how many. By the time of Noah, it seems, there was a sizeable population on the earth. Until the time of Noah, we have very little information other than what was related to the direct bloodline of Seth.

The Bloodline of Seth

Scripture has preserved for us the list of the descendants of Seth. I present it here in tabular form for handy reference. Of course, it is also preserved in Luke 3. The list below contains the ages for each fellow at the time of the birth of the key son in the generation after him. This is not necessarily, or even likely, the first son in the generation. It is the son who was, in a sense, the best *keeper of the culture* of Seth (really Adam) to pass on to future generations. The total lifespan of each gentleman is also provided.

- [Adam was 130 when Seth was born. Adam then lived to be 930. (130, 930)]
- **Seth** was 105 when Enosh was born, and lived 912 years. (105, 912)
- Enosh (90, 905)
- Kenan (70, 910)
- Mahalel (65, 895)
- Jared (162, 962)
- Enoch (65, 365) The text strongly implies that Enoch *did not die*.[18]
- Methuselah (187, 969) The longest-lived person in the Bible.
- Lamech (182, 777) Not the same man as the double-murderer in Cain's line.
- Noah (500, 950)

These fellows, each in his own turn, held the place for whomever was to come. In time, this would be reflected in the patriarchal prophecy Jacob bestowed on Judah (Gen. 49:10). They were not messiah *per se*, but marked His place until He came.

Their Wives

Let's just get right to it. Cain must have had a wife when he left Eden, or else he would have been alone in the world. Some want Cain to have found his wife after he left. But where would he find her? His parents were the two original persons. Unless GOD did the Adam and Eve thing multiple times, we have no place to find wives for the sons of Adam and Eve other than from among the daughters of Adam and Eve. This upsets us a lot. Incest is a very strong taboo. In fact, it was specified as such in the Law of Moses (Lev. 18:9). At the same time, when there are no other people from whom new people can come, we have to face this as the likely source of wives for the sons of the first generations. In a while, the women could be cousins or nieces even more remote in kinship, and then we all feel better.

There is a strong biological argument against incest, in that it highlights defective genes. Adam and Eve had no defective genes. The first generations were probably virtually defect-free. In a few generations, the choices were not so closely related and our concerns can soften. Even if there was intermarriage between the race of Cain and the race of Seth, there still had to be wives for Cain and Seth to begin with.[19] Sons and daughters were specified as having been born in each generation. Things soon got to what we are more accustomed to.

Abram was married to his half-sister, Sarai (Gen. 20:12-16). A few generations later, in the same culture, this became forbidden. It behooves us to face scripture squarely, as it is at odds with our modern context.

---

[1] The "curse" focused on the suitability of the ground for the growing of food. In particular, it appears that plant life that would not provide food would begin to come forth; things like thorns and brambles. It is possible that the ground itself began to change. Perhaps deserts began to appear. However, it is unlikely that significant tectonic forces began to occur. That seems relegated to the time of the flood. Think of that. Plant genetics began to "deteriorate" after the fall. Nutrients in the soil began to be "poorer" and so forth. Previously, the soil had been perfect and all plants produced useful food. While these statements are inferences, they seem accurate in light of the text itself (see Gen. 1:30). There seems to have been a perfect environment for useful plants at the end of creation. Furthermore, there was nothing harmful to that balance in The Creation. It was the curse that changed things. Perfect balance was originally the

order of the day in nature. The fall of Man resulted in those forces that brought disharmony into the creation, particularly with respect to plants and plant-based foods.

[2] James 3:16 tells us that self-will leads to chaos and wickedness. Certainly, the desire to "be like God" was a matter of self-will. The curse (Gen. 3:17-19) that caused the ground to not yield perfect crops was an early manifestation of chaos.

[3] When we consider the doom of Cain, it seems clear that he was exiled even from Eden. What had been possible in the garden in Eden faded in Eden after the exile of Adam. However, Eden was still holy whereas the rest of the continent was less blessed in some sense, even resulting in harsh conditions for Cain and his descendants.

[4] Cain means "to attain," which does suggest he was her first son. Cain would "establish" the family of Adam and Eve in their minds. These things do suggest he was their firstborn son.

[5] For example, they needed to replenish their loin coverings with new animal skins. This could be an occasion for a sacrificial event in which the life of the animal was offered up to GOD in thanks for His teaching them what covering was appropriate. The animal metaphorically covered their sin (manifested in shame for their physical nakedness). There being no other particular purpose for killing the animal (they were vegetarians as far as we can tell), the death of the skin-bearing animal would be seen as a holy event. The blood of the animal, then, prefigures the blood of JESUS as a redemption.

[6] Previously, they had only to pick food from trees. Now, because of the curse on the ground, they had to coax food to come forth. They had to toil for their food. As some animal products were also used as food, the brothers were offering back to GOD from the blessing of productivity that He provided them. It may be that predator and prey relationships were also direct results of the curse on the ground. In that case, husbandry would include protection for the animals that produced milk, cheese, and skins. Isaiah 11:6-7 and 65:25 suggest there will be an end of predation eventually, perhaps with the revealing of the sons of GOD.

[7] The *tithe* is not mentioned until we come to the context of Abram and Melchizedek in Genesis 14:18-20. These sacrifices appear to be precursors to the tithe. In Levitical times, sacrifices were the method of reconciliation, and tithing was also tied to agricultural success. In a non-monetary society, both tithes and offerings would be found in the form of sacrifices, as sacrifices were made of that which was produced through agricultural activity. The book of Leviticus is devoted to explaining these things in great detail in the context of the Aaronic priesthood.

[8] The fat portions seem to imply richness. Animals that were well-tended and in good health were the ones that produced a lot of fat. This signified not only the firstborn but also the best of the herds. This distinction would be much more difficult with plant products.

[9] C. Gaulden, *Birth of The Holy Nation, volume 1*, (Chambersburg, PA: eGen, 2015) offers a much fuller discussion of this matter in chapter 7.

[10] Matthew 23:35 and Hebrews 11:4 make this clear. His sacrifice was accepted when his brother's was not. When Eve bore Seth, she honored Abel (Gen. 4:25), even though Cain had been her firstborn.

[11] This analysis suggests that Adam and Eve were in Eden, but not in the garden, and that Cain had to leave Eden for elsewhere in the world. "Elsewhere" was not blessed by the special attention of GOD as was Eden. Adam and Eve remained in the holy place, while Cain was banished to another place. In turn, this suggests that Seth remained in Eden. So did his descendants down to Noah. See chapter 8 for a more detailed discussion of this.

[12] This probably means that Cain was made to look different than Seth and his descendants. One train of thought is that Cain was modified into something like one of the other supposed forms of human such as *Cro Magnon*, or some such. This could have resulted in significant genetic chaos among the descendants of Cain. Such chaos might well have resulted in a number of manifestations that were noticeably different from the descendants of Seth. In Eden, on the other hand, there likely remained orderly genetic

change. Chaotic change in Cain and his descendants would be accompanied by chaotic genetic changes in animals and plants outside of Eden as well. The flood in the time of Noah would erase that biological chaos but inter-marriage would then affect mankind after the flood. The curse on the ground for Adam's sake was of momentous importance in this scenario.

[13] The ground was cursed for Adam's sake (because of Adam). It was being "subjected to futility" (Rom. 8:20). This futility was to be progressive. For example, the flood of Noah's time would result in tectonic chaos with resultant deserts, volcanism, weather extremes, and so forth. These will continue progressively until the sons of GOD are revealed (Rev. 6:12, for example). This is not the desire of The Creation; it is the progressive breaking of the earth because of the sin of Adam.

[14] At the risk of offending our sensibilities concerning incest, there was not a large pool of women from which Cain could have selected a wife. On the other hand, the human genetic material had little by way of defect in it at that time. Other theories suggest there were multiple pockets of humanity besides Adam and Eve. The plain sense of the text tells us otherwise.

[15] Cain's murder of Abel would not fall from the memory of the rest of the family. The "marking" of Cain would keep that memory alive. In a sense, Cain's descendants and the other descendants of Adam (through Seth) would become two distinct peoples separated both genetically and geographically. Later we will distinguish them as Sethites and Cainites.

[16] While there were physical (genetic) differences, the real difference was spiritual. Cain "became" Cain by virtue of a curse GOD pronounced on him after he murdered Abel. The physical distinction is only a shadow of the spiritual difference.

[17] Melchizedek was a priest by scriptural declaration. He was in the spiritual line from Seth to JESUS. He was the same person as Shem. Priests are keepers of the faith and truth. In a sense, priests are micro-viceroys of GOD.

[18] It appears Enoch was translated rather than dying a natural death. This seems to have been a result of his status as a special "friend" of GOD.

[19] A straightforward reading of the text suggests there was only one Adam, not many. This, in turn, suggests the first generation had only siblings in the pool of potential spouses.

CHAPTER EIGHT

THE "RACES" OF SETH AND CAIN

We have examined the earliest generations of mankind as presented in scripture. In so doing, we found two bloodlines: that of Cain and that of Seth. The bloodline of Seth would have been Abel's bloodline had Cain not murdered Abel. This is made clear by the Eve's declaration in Genesis 4:25, in which she referred to Seth as a *replacement* for Abel. Cain, on the other hand, was specifically cursed by GOD after he had killed his brother (Gen. 4:11). There can be little doubt then that Seth's bloodline was in a more favorable posture with GOD than was Cain's bloodline. As such it is more central to scripture and more of its details are preserved for us.

For the sake of convenience and brevity I will use the phrases "**race of Seth**" and "**race of Cain**" to refer to these two bloodlines. The term "*race*" is laden with serious sociological and political overtones, but I will use the term nonetheless. In the specific context of this study, these two "races" refer not to ethnicity but to two general spiritual lineages. The **race of Cain** was birthed in fratricide that resulted in the eradication of identity. By contrast, the **race of Seth** was birthed in substitution.[1] These are two opposite and opposed spiritual trajectories.

In the previous chapter we delineated these two lines insofar as their first several natural generations are concerned. Scripture provides considerably more detail on the **race of Seth** than that of Cain. The reason is simple: Seth's bloodline is of much more moment to sacred history. This bloodline, which is at the core of the **race of Seth**, is the bloodline through which JESUS, the Son of GOD, came to the earth when He was born in the flesh (Lk. 3:23-38). In this sense, the **race of Seth** is a natural race determined by its spiritual properties. The bloodline of Cain has nothing to do with the genealogy of JESUS, either natural or spiritual. This is not to say that descendants of Cain could not access redemption. However, as we shall see, this "race" is reckoned to be erased in the Noahic flood, leaving marks, to be sure, on the **race of Seth**, but no longer distinctly present after the flood. Of course, the impact of Cain's (and Adam's) sins remained to plague the **race of Seth**. It was to the infected **race of Seth** that the invitation of redemption was to be given. Seth was a firstfruit of substitutionary redemption and JESUS was its culmination.

It is only fair to point out that after the end of the race and line of Cain at the time of the flood, Adam was the first father of the line of Seth, and Seth's was the only line to consider. From the time of the flood, we might reckon that Adam was the one from whom the lineage was to be reckoned. However, during the time in which the **race of Cain** was still in the earth, Adam was the father of both lineages. In the *bloodline* of the ancestors of JESUS, Adam is in fact present (Lk. 3:38). Furthermore, it was to Adam that the *death nature* of man was ascribed (1 Cor. 15:22). So all humans, even those of the extinct **race of Cain**, are descended from Adam with this death nature in tow. It was in CHRIST that the death nature itself was put to death. That nature affected the whole of humanity, the **race of Cain** and the **race of Seth** as well. Subsequent to the time of CHRIST, the inevitability of the death nature is set aside for all those who receive the work of redemption through faith in Christ.

However, for the moment, we will not use a term like **race of Adam** because it would not enable us to clearly negotiate the events that precipitated the flood. We need to continue to distinguish the bloodline and **race of Seth** from the **race of Cain** to properly navigate the flood narrative. Again, keep in mind, the real importance of the terms is a spiritual distinction.[2] After the flood, the term **race of Adam** would simply be of no real value because it would not distinguish anything. From that point on it is virtually the same as the **race of Seth** for us. It is essentially synonymous with mankind.

Keep in mind the term **race of Seth** is not a biblical term. I am using it in this study for the specific purpose of distinguishing the two branches of mankind after the time of the brief occupancy of the garden in Eden. We need to keep in mind that the **race of Seth** remained in Eden (not the garden) even after GOD expelled the **race of Cain**.

Priesthood Begins

I think it prudent at this point to explain a very important aspect of the lineage we have been discussing: the origin of the priesthood. While a study of the full topic itself exceeds the scope of this book, a brief overview will help us understand the importance of this "eternal" phenomenon, how it developed in parallel with and relates to the ongoing development and history of the **race of Seth.**

After Moses and the Israelites left Egypt, they soon came to the area of Mount Sinai. In fact, it was three months to the day after leaving Egypt.[3] They had a few adventures along the way, but Sinai was their first primary destination (Ex. 3:12). Indeed, they spent almost a year at Mount Sinai, receiving the Law from GOD, building the Tabernacle, and launching the liturgy. When all was in order, they departed from Mount Sinai one year, one month and five days after leaving Egypt. When they set out, the newly ordained Aaronic priests and the Levites were charged with the care of the newly finished and dedicated Tabernacle. This was the launching of the priesthood of Aaron and his descendants.[4] So the Aaronic (also called Levitical) priesthood was launched in the context of the nation setting forth with its defining legislation and liturgical accoutrements.

Some number of days before the Lord specified that Aaron and his descendants were to "occupy" a priesthood (Ex. 28:1-4), however, He instructed Moses to caution the people to exercise great care regarding their behavior whenever He came down to speak to them. Specifically, they were to consecrate themselves in advance and carefully observe the boundary of their approach: they were not to touch or set foot on the mountain (Ex. 19:12, 22-24). Twice in His instructions to Moses GOD used the term "the priests" in such a way as to make a distinction between them and the rest of the people. This distinction was very important from GOD's perspective. For one thing, "the priests" were required to consecrate themselves a third time before coming up to the boundary.[5] Both "the priests" and "the people" were to observe the boundary when they got there. This may only be a casual distinction, but it does not appear to be casual. Among the people was a subset which could be referred to as "the priests." In this address to Moses, GOD made it clear that "the priests," while they were among the people, were in that setting distinguished from the rest of "the people." However that distinction was to be understood, it mattered in this instance.

Two days prior to introducing this distinction, the Lord GOD had said to Moses that He desired for "the people" to be a "*kingdom of priests and a holy nation*" (Ex. 19:6). This passage implies that GOD wanted *all* the people to be "priests" in some sense. If all the people were "priests," it would make no sense to distinguish between "the people" and "the priests," even in conversation. Either designation would apply to all of them equally.

For some reason, then, the group designated as "the priests" were differentiated from the rest of "the people" in the eyes of GOD by the time the Israelites arrived at Mount Sinai. Moses was to consecrate all the people on two days in a row to ready them for the conference with GOD on the third day. On the third day, this subset of "the people" GOD called "the priests" was to engage in a third consecration in addition to the two conducted by Moses. Whoever "the priests" were, they were capable or worthy in some sense to consecrate themselves in an act that distinguished them from the rest of "the people." After the Israelites departed from Mount Sinai, the term "priest" applied only to Aaron and his descendants. The obvious question now is, who were these Israelites that GOD called "the priests" at Mount Sinai *before* the specific designation of the Aaronic priests by ordination?

A superficial reading of Exodus 19 suggests that they are Aaron and his sons. This is unlikely, however, because at that time no specific indication of their selection had yet been made. While Aaron was in a noticeably unique position as Moses' spokesperson (Ex. 4:14-16), he had not yet been called "priest." Even more cogently, Aaron and his sons had not been *ordained* as priests. While that would occur in relatively short order, it still was almost a year away. To identify Aaron and his sons as priests so early in the affairs of the nation risks downplaying the importance of GOD's expressed desire that all "the people" would be priests (Ex. 19:6).

It is very unlikely that priests of any other religious order existed among the people. While the people likely had some worshippers of various Egyptian gods in their midst, it is hard to imagine GOD paying any particular notice of them other than to discourage the continuation of their practices. Furthermore, it is also highly unlikely that the Egyptians would have allowed any formal Israelite involvement in their religious system. In fact, the Egyptian priests were a particular category of people in a formal sense (Gen. 47:20-22). Most significantly, it was to GOD that the Israelites had called out in their distress in Egypt. When they departed from that land under Moses, some Egyptians went with them, but even if there were priests among them, it is, again, very unlikely that the Lord would have recognized any of those priests in a positive way.

Who Were These Priests?

Again, who were these "priests" among "the people?" I propose there were certain persons among the people as a whole who were recognized as having a particularly close relationship with GOD. In virtually every religion, there are those who simply adhere more closely to the things of their deity than do the rank and file of the people. No doubt, there were those among the Israelites in Egypt who were recognized as being more devoted to GOD. These "devout" individuals may often have been the objects of derision for some, enduring hostility of varying degrees of intensity. Most of us know how it feels to be mocked or sneered at by people who accuse us of having a "holier than thou" attitude. This is, of course, a very ambiguous distinction. There can be little reasonable doubt, though, that some people in every generation have always been more devoted to the things of GOD than others. Perhaps there was even some sort of unspoken agreement among the various Israelite families that old cousin so-and-so would be all right with being called a "priest" and could be counted on if the rest of the family needed to know something from GOD.

In any event, the concept of the priest was known among the people. Otherwise, they would not have understood the instructions. Apparently, "the people" and "the priests" and Moses knew what was meant.

Let's back up several centuries. A few years after Abram moved to Canaan, certainly well before he came to be known as Abraham, he had a meeting with a fellow named Melchizedek (Gen. 14:18-20).[6] The biblical narrative specifies that Melchizedek was "a priest of God Most High" (Gen. 14:18). This begs the question, how could that be? Who made that designation? Even stranger, how is it he was *a* priest and not *the* priest of GOD Most High? Was he a priest of some other GOD in addition to the Lord GOD? The extensive development of the nature of his priesthood in the book of Hebrews makes it very clear that Melchizedek was a priest of Our Father and not some other GOD (Heb. 5:1–7:28). That rather lengthy passage makes it very clear that this fellow Melchizedek was a priest of GOD Most High hundreds of years before the events at Mount Sinai.

The point is that some persons were referred to as priests of the Lord GOD long before Aaron was born. Aaron and his descendants occupied a very formal priesthood that dated from the building and dedication of the Tabernacle at Mount Sinai. About the physical accoutrements of this fellow Melchizedek we know nothing except that he prophesied to Abram in GOD's name and that he brought the elements of what we know as communion to share with Abram. He received a tithe from Abram as well. This was not a Levitical event. This priesthood, which is further attested in the Hebrews passage, was quite unlike the Aaronic priesthood. Nonetheless, Melchizedek was a worthy priest of GOD Most High there in Canaan when it was a very pagan place.

If there was this one priest hundreds of years before Aaron, might there have been others? Of course there were. Had Melchizedek been unique in the earth, then his priesthood would have been presented with an explanation as to how it came about. A reasonable consideration of his situation leads to the conclusion that priests of GOD Most High have existed through the ages.

What Do Priests Do?

We haven't yet asked ourselves about what priests do. In the Levitical system their duties were well and formally described. As we have just seen, we can assess Melchizedek's priestly functions fairly well simply by observing a single event. Nonetheless, Abram knew who he was and accepted his primacy. Hence the tithe.

When considering the formal definition of the term priest, we must be careful not to be too narrow in our thinking or we may miss some of the broader parameters. Technically, a priest is one who serves a primarily medial role. In a sense, Melchizedek *mediated* between GOD and Abram, for example. His mediation took three forms. First, he blessed Abram in the name of GOD. Apparently, he was authorized by GOD to do so, and apparently Abram recognized that authority. Second, he served a symbolic meal to Abram in a format that Abram accepted as legitimate. Third, he accepted a tithe from Abram on GOD's behalf. We can safely conclude that he "mediated" between GOD and Abram.[7]

The First Temple

We saw in an earlier chapter that Eden served as a "holy" place and of the garden in Eden as a "most holy" place. In that sense, Eden was the first type of the temple of God to be found in the Tabernacle, the Jerusalem temple, and the temple of the New Jerusalem. The latter, the temple of the New Jerusalem that came down out of heaven (Third Heaven), was not actually a physical temple. The "traditional" temple was unnecessary because God and the Lamb are its temple (Rev. 21:22). There can be little doubt that the New Jerusalem that descended in the visions of John was a city that originated in Third Heaven. In Third Heaven, there is a throne at the center of things. We can readily extrapolate from these facts that the temple is not the focal point in Third Heaven for the same reason: God Almighty and His Lamb are there. There is no need for a temple because the acts of mediation are not necessary when we are in Third Heaven. Mediation is ended when we enter there because mediation is only needed when there is separation. Mediation is a sort of bridge.

In John's vision, he was in a place where mediation was celebrated as completed in the song of the elders and the four living beings (Rev. 5:9-10). Mediation was finished so that, among other things, the Lamb (Jesus) was qualified to take the book and open the seals that had previously held it shut. In Third Heaven, then, no temple was needed because the temple was the place where the priests performed whatever acts of mediation were necessary or prescribed, and that was no longer necessary.

What has that to do with Eden? The garden in Eden was apparently the place of fellowship between God and Adam and Eve. God would visit the garden but Adam was to tend the garden. In those services, Adam figuratively was tending to that which related the earth to its Creator. Following this reasoning, Adam acted as a priest on behalf of The Creation (at least its earth component). The first instance of this was the naming of the animals (Gen. 2:19). In so doing, he figuratively represented their interests with God. In a sense, he was introducing the various animals to God in their actual identities. This act solidified the identity of each animal and its relationship to its Creator.

Adam the Priest

Nowhere in scripture is Adam called a priest. As we have just seen though, it is not hard to understand that he *acted as a priest* as long as he was in the garden in Eden. The garden, as we have seen, was a "most holy" place. This is equivalent to the "holy of holies" behind the veil in the later Tabernacle and temple. Adam functioned in that place as a priest. In a sense, the interests of The Creation were in his hands. At the same time, he represented GOD to the Creation. That was the mediational position he occupied.

What about Adam after the fall? At the time of the fall, there was no other man in the world who could take up the responsibilities of the priest. While he could no longer go into the garden (most holy place), he seems to have remained in Eden itself, which, as we have seen, was a "holy" place. In the temple-to-come, this was the place outside the veil through which one passed to enter the most holy place. In the "holy place" the whole cast of priests could perform the various functions other than those which only the most holy place could host. Adam, as priest, could still function as priest in Eden. I believe that Adam continued to be a priest to GOD in spite of the instance of his fall.

What might Adam have done as a priest after his expulsion from the garden? In him was all of the knowledge of GOD. He could maintain that knowledge and he could pass it on to his sons. There can be little doubt that he passed on the knowledge of GOD to his sons. In the story of Cain and Abel, we see that both of these sons of Adam knew to bring sacrifices to GOD (Genesis 4:3-5). It is also apparent from the passage that Abel retained better what his father had taught him. He knew to bring the firstlings for offerings and did so. If Abel knew to bring the first fruits of his labor, then it seems unreasonable to assume that Cain did not know it. Between the two of them, then, Abel had *the better sacrifice* and this caused Cain to hate him out of envy. He even denied his role as elder brother in the process (Gen. 4:9).

157

The "Line" of Priests

The text highlights the fact that Seth replaced Abel in the family (Gen. 4:25-26), probably the next born after the murder of Abel and expulsion of Cain from Eden. Seth was not likely the only other son born to Adam and Eve. It is quite likely that quite a few other sons followed. GOD was, after all, causing the earth to be occupied by humans. In time, Seth also began to produce sons. In particular, he had a son named Enosh (Gen. 4:26). This verse contains a remarkable statement. It says that in the lifetime of Enosh, they "began to call upon the name of the Lord" (Gen. 4:26). In the time of Enosh, the knowledge of GOD began to include some kind of worship in addition to the offering up of sacrifices of first fruits.[8]

The fifth chapter of Genesis lists a genealogy that specifies one particular son in each generation of direct lineage from Seth. In each generation there were other sons, likely many other sons. In each generation, there was one man who was known to be the one who was a kind of "keeper of the relationship" between GOD and the other people who were alive in the time. By setting aside one son in each generation, GOD was insuring the eternal continuity of awareness of who He was and who they were in Him. This man, I believe, was responsible before GOD with the preservation of the authentic knowledge. He represented GOD to his generation. Thus, each generation was assured access to GOD in some sense.

Now Adam did not die until there were eight succeeding generations in the earth. Adam, then, was the main authority for a very long time. But Adam came along when he did. His son Seth was his guaranty of continuity beyond the grave.[9] In turn, Enosh was the guaranty of Seth's continuity beyond the grave, and so forth through each generation. Each generation was the guaranty of eternity for its parent generation. So even though these men lived for many generations in the earliest days, the guaranty was in the son and not in the generations after the son. It was therefore necessary that there be a designated guaranty in each generation. Those men are listed in the fifth chapter of Genesis.

Each one was the primary priest in his generation. Priesthood, then, was a generational phenomenon. Even if a father outlived his son, that son was his guaranty. Only in the event of the death of a man's son could he change that guaranty, and then only by an adoption of the grandson to replace the son, even if the adoption were informal in nature. GOD would not have a generation without a priest to stand before Him to represent that generation. In that way no generation could claim to be omitted from GOD's workings in the earth.

It is interesting that the lineal heritage of JESUS included each of these key sons from the earliest days (Lk. 3:23-38). JESUS never married nor did He have natural sons. The line was broken in Him in that sense. JESUS, however, *being eternal*, did not need a guaranty. He was the guaranty for the Eternal Father. He was, in a very real and eternal sense, the guaranty for all generations to come. After Him there was no need for the guaranty to be traced any longer. This is a key conclusion of the Hebrews account of Melchizedek (Heb. 7:17, 21). He was a "priest forever." He was the "*high* priest forever according to the order of Melchizedek" (Heb. 6:20, emphasis added).

The function of priest requires a constant presence. Mankind is mortal. GOD, therefore, saw to it that there was always a priest to represent Him in some degree until *the eternal high priest* came. This was not a late innovation. It began in the garden in Eden and continued in every generation, reaching its apogee in JESUS, who remains the eternal priest and high priest. The tree of life, which was lost to man when he was exiled from the garden in Eden, is to be recovered when the new Jerusalem descends to the earth when the works of redemption are finished (Rev. 22:1-2).

The Priest Abraham

It has been said and widely accepted that Abram was a heathen and that GOD had to work with him a long time before he could be qualified to be called Abraham. The line of priests, however, contains the name of Abraham right between those of Terah (his father) and

Isaac (his son). I believe Abraham was the priest to his generation of the descendants of Seth and sons of GOD. He knew Melchizedek because Melchizedek was a priest in the same lineage from ten generations earlier.[10]

We should note that Joshua 24:2 implies that Abraham might have been a polytheist before he went to Canaan. If the story of Laban and his "household gods" (Gen. 31:30) is any indication, Abraham's relatives who remained in Aram Nahoraim continued in that tradition. Nevertheless, I still maintain that Abram was selected as the priest of his generation even if Terah by that time had greatly diluted the knowledge of the true God.

Isaac was a priest after Abraham. Jacob became the priest of his generation after Isaac. These men were the representative priests, each in his own generation. Surely, though, among the thousands of Israelites in Egypt, there were others who could be counted on to know GOD. In the time of Jacob, the one man was becoming a nation in which the knowledge of GOD would be widespread. In the following generations, there would be many who could be called "priest" in each generation. Yes, there would be only one man in each generation in the direct ancestral line of JESUS, but there were likely many who were priests in the sense we have discussed.

There has always been at least one priest in every generation to represent the interests of GOD to the persons in that generation. There is one high priest, and only one, whom we must view as the original, primal priest. That one is JESUS, and since His time in the earth we have had a proper explanation and understanding of that reality. Nonetheless, from the earliest time there have been priests of the order of which He is the High Priest. That order is not otherwise represented in the earth, even though there have been many priesthoods that have emerged. Still, there is only the one priesthood that is eternal as described in the song of the elders and living creatures offered up at the throne in Third Heaven (Rev. 4:9-10). Adam and Abraham were priests in this order. In time, that whole nation will be composed of priests who are also of royal spiritual lineage.

The Provocation

Let's be clear that the flood that occurred in the time of Noah was inevitable. This was unknown to the inhabitants of the earth, kept only in the counsels of the Godhead until such time that GOD chose to make it known to a man. But it became inevitable.

We cannot know what happened to the knowledge of GOD among those who were of the **race of Cain**. It seems fair to suggest that Cain came to recall GOD very differently than did Adam. Adam had sinned, of course. But Cain had murdered and was exiled to a place even further away from the first home (in the garden in Eden). In fact, Cain had never even seen the garden in Eden. Also, the ground had been cursed because of Adam, but Cain was "the cursed one" after his infraction. The ground was cursed because of Adam (Gen. 3:17), but Cain was cursed from the ground (Gen. 4:11). Cain was cursed from that which was cursed. We might view this as a sort of double-curse. Such a man probably would never be at peace with GOD again. Hence, his views of GOD came to be distorted from reality in such a way as to provide a quite deficient view of GOD. Consequently, whatever he taught his sons about GOD after the curse would be inaccurate—and stray farther from the truth with every generation. Scripture suggests that Cain had no sons until after his exile had commenced.

Adam, on the other hand, seems to have repented of his infraction. This is indicated by the fact that, in the bloodline of Seth, a man as pure as Enoch, and another as pure as Noah, were to be found. This might relate to the fact that the exile of Cain separated him from his father and mother, whereas Seth, as far as we know, remained in close contact with them.

If we could compare side-by-side the worldviews of a person in Cain's bloodline and a person in Seth's bloodline, even a short time after the exile, we probably would find the differences striking. It would never happen, however, because the mark that GOD put on Cain probably would prohibit such a meeting. Hence, as time went on the knowledge of GOD became seriously distorted among the descendants of Cain. In contrast, it seems safe to assume that Enoch (the Seth-ite) was a man who had a highly accurate knowledge of GOD.[11] This implies that Seth's line was more diligent to remember GOD as He had revealed Himself to Adam. The guiding viewpoint for this study, as previously discussed, is that the bloodline of Seth down to Noah was composed of the men in each generation who were noted (possibly even formally) to have best kept the knowledge of GOD as passed down from Adam to Seth and on down the line. Actually, Adam was still alive when Enoch was born.[12] In fact, Adam died during the lifetime of Lamech, the father of Noah, only 131 years before Noah was born. Think of that; Noah would be the first man in the direct bloodline from Adam to JESUS to not have been alive during Adam's lifetime. By the way, Methuselah died at about the same time as the flood–perhaps in the flood–but more likely his death "permitted" the flood.

It may seem arbitrary to some, but let's suppose we can call the named man in each generation a kind of provisional high-priest. (To others this may even seem presumptuous.) However, it would have been in the interest of Seth, for example, to find a son of his whom he could train to bear such a load in the event of Seth's death. It seems unlikely that Seth could have known what his lifespan would actually be. Nor would he know that Adam would live so long. As far as he knew, Adam would die and it would be up to him to keep alive the memory of GOD. Then, in time, his son might be the one who would have to keep that information accurate. Adam surely told Seth that he was under a death sentence since that day at the **tree of the knowledge of good and evil**. At the same time, Seth certainly would have witnessed multiple times the deaths of animals. He knew of death well enough to recognize the importance of making careful advance preparations, including passing on spiritual leadership of the **race of Seth** to some specific person for the sake of continuity.

It is highly likely that each man in his turn was trained by his father specifically to pick up the spiritual leadership of the people when his father died. This training might even have been at the hands of the oldest ancestor still alive at the time. Something this important would not have been left to chance. It seems reasonable to think that written records came into being fairly soon after the garden expulsion. These fellows seem to be the likely keepers of those records as well.

Logically, the separation between the **race of Seth** and the **race of Cain** would have been such as to make interaction between the two "peoples" much rarer than interactions within each group. The curse of Cain "from the ground," along with a wandering existence, underlay the relative separation between the two groups of people. Cain also lived outside the context of Eden by GOD's decree. And the mark of Cain, whatever it was, likely reinforced reticence among the two peoples to have very much to do with one another.[13] These phenomena gave rise to a more-or-less natural divide between the two groups.

Let's establish some working definitions at this point. For reasons of which we are unaware, the chronicler of the phase of history in question used the word "**men**" in a limited way.[14] The chronicler also makes special usage of the term "**sons of God**" alongside the use of "men."[15] In the early part of Genesis chapter 6, the term "man" seems to be used in reference to the descendants of Cain. This conclusion derives from the fact that the term "sons of God" is used in contradistinction to it. One was either a "man" or a "son of God" in this passage, but not both.[16] That being the case, the daughters that were born to the category "men" were descendants of Cain along with their fathers and brothers. If the term "sons of God" is used in this instance to distinguish these fellows from the descendants of Cain, then they are of the **race of Seth**. This use of the term "sons of God" is unique, by the way. The term is not used in this manner anywhere else in scripture. In this special usage:

"men" = descendants of Cain

"sons of GOD" = descendants of Seth.

In light of these equivalencies, the passage in question (Gen. 6:1-4) states that some males among the descendants of Seth took wives for themselves from among the descendants of Cain. The passage is quite specific in that sense. It does not state, for example, that descendants of Cain took wives from among the descendants of Seth. The unusual specificity of the language makes the latter case unlikely.

Let's keep in mind that we are using these natural phenomena to help us understand spiritual matters. In any particular family, be it of Cainites (**race of Cain**) or Sethites (**race of Seth**), the responsibility for the family fell on the male in his capacities as husband and father. It did not fall on the female. So the specification of gender in the passage is important. A male Sethite had the paternal responsibility for his family. A female Sethite did not have such responsibility. At the same time, a male Cainite would have paternal responsibility for his family, but not a female Cainite. Hence, if such a person married a female Sethite, her original identity would be surrendered and she would be reckoned to be a Cainite. The husband's identity would determine the spiritual "identity" of the family. No mention is made of male Cainites marrying female Sethites in the narrative, however. This would likely be unthinkable among the descendants of Seth. On the other hand, they might rationalize the marriage of male descendants of Seth to female descendants of Cain because the weight of identity and responsibility would go to the husband anyway. These considerations may be inaccurate in specific cases but seem generally to capture what was going on.

The passage strongly implies that GOD was offended by this phenomenon. By extension, He did not intend that "sons of God" (descendants of Seth) should marry women from among "men" (descendants of Cain). It is not at all clear how the descendants of Seth would know of this prohibition, but they must have or GOD would not have held them guilty of transgressing the prohibition. This, then, is the provocation, that descendants of Seth married women descended from Cain.

What was the problem with that? The Cainite woman would be married to the Sethite man and become a Sethite in the process. However, she would remember her natural family and its practices, including its religion. On occasion, in fact, she might bring up their cultural differences in disputes with her husband. In many cases, she would likely secretly teach her children these alien ideas and practices. In some sense, this could result in a significant pollution of the knowledge of GOD among the **race of Seth**. The largely compromised knowledge of GOD that was found among the descendants of Seth would then lead to ambiguity and insecurity among them.[17] As a result, strange beliefs and practices might well emerge (see Rev. 2:14 for example). In such a matrix such practices as child sacrifice might come into being accompanied by a sometimes sincere belief that GOD (by some other name, like Chemosh) was behind it. GOD would not be mocked (Gal. 6:7) in these deceptions, however.

At a spiritual level, the women who were descended from Cain would introduce the unholy into the holy place in these marriages. That would certainly displease GOD. He had separated Cain from the rest of Adam's offspring for a reason.

Again, how would the men of the **race of Seth** know there was a prohibition in this matter? We simply do not know, but they did. GOD would not have left such a thing to chance. The whole Bible, in fact, is part of the manifestation of the fact that GOD does not take such things for granted. When Sethite men married Cainite women, they knew it was displeasing to GOD. It is likely, given the importance of the matter, that GOD specifically informed one or more of the "sons of God" so as to make it clear that the separation was His desire. At the same time, it is also likely that He did not inform "men" (descendants of Cain) because of the separation between Himself and them.

It is clear that GOD became provoked and that this particular phenomenon was a sort of touch-point for His displeasure (Gen. 6:5-7). Some read this passage to mean that GOD had made a mistake. It should not be read that way. When we choose to bring children into the world, we know they will grieve us in some instances but that does not cause us to fail to produce them, nor do we fail to love them when they do grieve us. It is also true that He set out to preserve humans for the future after He had made the adjustments He found necessary.

That GOD repented from making man (Gen. 6:6) has long been considered a confusing passage. However, if the reference is to the **race of Cain** instead of all mankind, the passage is clearer. He would eradicate that line but preserve the **race of Seth**. While this may not be what the passage means, it does provide for a clear delineation.

"Found Favor"

At the time GOD began to take action to bring judgment on mankind, He also identified His own vessel of preservation for the work He had begun in Eden. He would keep a man and his wife safe from the coming wrath. Furthermore, He would preserve the lives of their sons and their son's wives. In so doing, He assured the repopulation of the earth with humans after the time of judgment had ended. In fact, He went so far as to assure the reproductive lives of the animals in the earth. This was to be a "resurrected" creation, not a new one. It was to come out of a kind of baptism.

One man, a man in the bloodline that connects Seth to JESUS, was identified as worthy of survival. That man was the son of Lamech, who had emerged as the most GOD-like of the men in his generation. This fellow, Noah, was directly descended naturally and spiritually from his ancestor Seth. Interestingly, Noah's birth was really but a short time after the death of Seth–only 14 years.

The spiritual ambiguity of Cain and his descendants likely was reflected in a kind of physical ambiguity (the mark of Cain) as well (see endnote 13). There probably was no "pure" doctrine or any person to keep track of such a doctrine among the descendants of Cain. A true doctrine of GOD was lost to Cain and his descendants after his murder of Abel. At the same time, and without forgetting the sin of Adam, the line of Adam through Seth seems to have remained more stable, both physically and spiritually. I understand this is a lot to take in and we do not want to form dogma here. This idea is only food for thought.

It is important to note that the passage does *not* say the Nephilim are the children of "sons of God" and daughters of "men." It only says they were around at the same time, whatever their origin. Some have suggested the passage makes the Nephilim out to be the offspring of the improper marriages. More likely, they were some sort of descendants of Cain and not found in the **race of Seth**. It also seems likely, in any event, that they were destroyed in the flood. At the same time, their genetic characteristics might well have come into the **race of Seth** by way of the Cainite women whom Seth's descendants married along the way.[18]

However these things happened, GOD was ready to bring about a type of redemption for mankind through the flood. And so He warned Noah, the *de-facto* priest in his generation. Noah's father, Lamech, and his grandfather, Methuselah, were both still alive at the time the warning was issued, but it was issued to Noah and not to one of them. Noah was the one chosen to carry the knowledge of GOD and to begin the work of rebuilding. He and his sons were to launch the new age of man. They were "sons of God" with the requisite knowledge and capacities to get the necessary work done.

The sons of Noah were Shem, Ham, and Japheth. This, however, was not their birth-order.[19] It was the order of their impact on sacred history. Shem carried on the lineage from Seth that led eventually to JESUS. Ham was the offender of his father. Japheth was just less prominent in the stories.

To the one who had found favor in the eyes of GOD, He now stated His decision along with the reason for it. He told Noah that the earth was filled with violence because of men and He was going to destroy men with the earth.[20] On the other hand, He would preserve a remnant through whom the earth would be repopulated.

Passenger Manifest

Almost everyone knows the story of Noah's ark.[21] It is one of the most prominent stories in the religious training of children, at least among Jewish and Christian children. The motif is so enhanced by the inclusion of animals among the passengers of the ark. In so many ways the ideas remain in common knowledge and the inclusion of animals is always paramount.

So what about the animals? GOD had specified which humans

were to be aboard the ark, but how were the animals to be included? The instructions were actually included in the commission GOD gave to Noah. *GOD would send animals to Noah for their inclusion.*[22] They would be sent; Noah would not have to go and gather them. In some manner, the senses of the specific animals to be included would be imbued with the necessity to show up at the right time. In this way, GOD would insure that the animals He wanted to be on the ark would be present. In fact, the correct numbers of each kind would show up: two pairs of unclean and seven pairs of clean animals. At the same time, if GOD did not send an animal to the ark, that one would not show up. Many folks are worried about such things as dinosaurs. The evidence for the existence of dinosaurs in the past is strong, but GOD was not compelled to send them to the ark. The language in scripture (Gen. 6:19-20) may sound like all species would show up. It does not, however, assign to Noah the task of gathering them. Hence, if GOD omitted to include some animals, that was His choice.[23] By the way, Noah was assigned the two tasks of building the ark and provisioning it. This was appropriate in that the man was the descendant of the first viceroy of GOD to the world. As such, he would naturally be expected to protect and provide for the inhabitants of the ark.[24] Clearly, Noah was now the representative of the Lord GOD in the earth, and he was the one through whom the survival of the earth and all that was in the earth depended.

"The Flood Came upon the Earth"

When the time came, the Lord sent Noah and his family into the ark and gave the animals time to arrive. After a week, the great flood began. Ordinarily, we focus on the rain that lasted for "forty days and forty nights" when we think about the flood narrative. Interestingly, the narrative first tells us that the *"fountains of the great deep burst open"* and then the *"floodgates of the sky were opened"* (Gen. 7:11). "Burst" is an interesting verb. It carries the strong connotation of violence. Something powerfully violent occurred. This was not some sort of small event. In the context of that action, enormous quantities of water found their way up from within the earth to its surface. This fundamentally changed the earth. No longer were great quantities of water confined to the interior; they were now loosed. In order for that to occur, the vast reservoirs of water that were within the earth vacated the caverns that contained them. In so doing, the containing formations began to break up. As this all happened in a very short period of time (forty days), the seismic disturbances must have been of such scale as we cannot easily imagine. The earth basically was physically broken. What we call "tectonic" activity occurred on a planetary scale and with such force that the whole face of land on the earth essentially was destroyed. The one landmass was forced apart into the many pieces we now call continents. It is likely that the proportion of the earth's surface now characterized by land is much higher. High mountain ranges were created by those forces. The oceans became much deeper. Nothing that was on the earth would likely have survived the sheer power of what was happening – and it went on for forty days and nights.

At the same time, *"the floodgates of the sky were opened."* This implies extraordinary rain. It seems reasonable to assume that the waters escaping from the earth were vaporized to a great extent in the initial releases. This, combined with the waters that were already above the earth, resulted in great volumes of rain.[25] The storms must have been beyond anything ever seen on the earth before or since. The disturbances from beneath and the movement of water vapors and rain in the atmosphere must have combined to produce storms that make our modern hurricanes and typhoons look tame. It is likely that a floating box was the only thing that could have survived these dynamics.

These great alterations probably left the earth in much the configuration which now exists. But they likely took place very quickly, in only a matter of days. Mankind was obliterated except for the two-generation family in the ark. The **race of Cain** was gone. Land-borne and airborne animals were obliterated except for those who had been sent to the ark. Other than the acts of creation, nothing so dramatic has ever occurred inside The Creation when viewed from a natural perspective. The earth itself was thoroughly altered in those few days. The outpouring of the water took forty days, but the alterations of the earth might well have taken considerably longer.

The only evidence of Cain was the likely presence of the spiritual memory of his greatly distorted religion that had been passed around in such a way as to have some level of conscious presence in the minds of Noah and his family. But mankind and the animals survived through their presence in the ark. After the flood was over, they began to reproduce as they had done before and the earth and atmosphere again became their homes.

It took a while, but the violent rearrangements of the earth finally came to an end. It may be that they continue in small measure until now because the earth cannot fully rest until the sons of GOD are finally revealed in the earth. But the major cataclysms ended and the waters that had been so forcibly poured out onto its surface began to find rest. The deeper places filled with water and the shallower places were uncovered. As a result, the surface of the earth emerged in roughly the configuration it now has. Since that time, changes in the earth have been much smaller and less violent than in the time of the flood. Even our great modern cataclysms are localized relative to the planet-wide violence of those few weeks and months. As GOD had told Noah, all the land and air animals and all of mankind that were not in the ark with him and his family were destroyed. There were no other survivors in the animal kingdom except waterborne animals.

The enormous forces of nature released in the earth in those days flooded the entire earth. As the convulsions tore the land areas apart and rearranged them, the waters piled up. When the violence was over, it was time to wait for the waters to find their new depths. This took a while. It is a property of water in its liquid form to find the lowest place it can get to. No matter how long it takes, it will continue to move as long as there is a path to a lower place.

In fact, the whole process from the beginning of the great fountains breaking forth and the rain beginning to fall until the ark came aground took exactly five months.[26] It took another two-and-a-half months, approximately, before the water had subsided enough that Noah and his family could see other mountains from the place where the ark was lodged. A bit more than another month (forty days) went by before Noah began to prepare for disembarking from the ark.

At that point, he sent out a raven to find evidence that the land was ready for the occupants of the ark to come out. The raven came and went for some number of days. Eventually, the raven found a place to "stay" and ceased coming back to the ark.[27] When the raven ceased coming back to the ark, Noah sent out a tenderer messenger to determine how things were progressing. The dove didn't like what she found outside and returned to the ark. A week later the process was repeated, but this time the dove came back with evidence of plant life (an olive twig). On her third weekly trip she simply did not return. Noah took this as the sign that life could again proceed on the face of the earth. At ten lunar months and thirteen days, Noah determined the earth was about ready for human and animal life again.

One year and ten days after the flooding began, GOD instructed Noah to disembark from the ark along with the rest of its inhabitants. Obviously, when they came out they were not where they had been when things started. Wherever it was, though, they must have been quite pleased to start this new phase of their lives. Noah offered up a sacrifice of every clean animal and bird pretty quickly. GOD made an oath to Himself that such things as had happened would not happen again in the earth. In some manner, He made known to Noah the contents of that eternally binding oath.[28] The text seems to imply that the sacrifices Noah offered up stimulated the oath.

Out of the Ark

Dry land must have looked really good to Noah's family and the animals after their long voyage to a place that may well not have existed when they went into the ark. Noah's thanksgiving sacrifice probably formally marked their gratitude and relief.

At that time, GOD charged Noah and his family with responsibility for the earth. This was basically the same charge as the one He gave Adam when he was created. There is a different tone, though. In this instance GOD speaks of fear. The animals would *fear* Noah and his descendants. Such was not the case at the beginning.[29]

We can ask ourselves about the distinction between clean and unclean animals. When Noah was welcoming animals into the ark before the flood, how did he distinguish? We may infer that he did not need to distinguish between the two categories. If seven pairs came to him for passage, they were clean. If only two pairs came, they were not clean. This enabled him to know what to sacrifice when they emerged from the ark. But GOD was now allowing him and his family to eat any animal they chose, unlike the prohibitions to appear later in Sinai.[30]

The Bow in the Sky

We typically call it a rainbow. It is quite interesting that GOD chose to provide a visual symbol from nature to remind Him and us of the covenant He first made with Himself (Gen. 8:21-22) and then with us through Noah (Gen. 9:11-17). Scripture specifies that He made this covenant with Himself after "smelling the soothing aroma" of the sacrifices provided by Noah at the time of disembarkation. GOD is, of course, not a corporeal being. "Smelling the soothing aroma" is likely a metaphorical expression to enable us to understand something about Him. The aroma was soothing to GOD in this metaphor. The question for us, then, must deal with how the aroma soothed Him. In the natural, the smell of flesh burning is not all that pleasant. So how did that soothe GOD? Perhaps He was soothed in the sense that Noah was voluntarily offering the sacrifice to Him. The flood itself had been the manifestation of GOD's wrath toward the persistent perversion of mankind. Now Noah was sacrificing out of appreciation for the providence and protection GOD had provided to him and his family.[31] It's as though GOD received Noah's sacrifices as an eternal intervention with GOD on behalf of man and the earth. This is particularly so because of the righteousness of Noah (Gen. 6:9).

These things did not fully restore the earth. It was still true that the sin-nature was in man as it had been since Adam and Eve failed in the garden. Consequently, a kind of downward trend in the natural creation is to continue throughout the ages until the sons of GOD are fully revealed (Rom. 8:18-25).[32] So predation began to happen in the earth. This will be reversed when the sons of GOD are fully revealed and predators and prey are reconciled (Is. 11:6-7). In fact, nature will return to a vegetarian state in which great predators will eat grains (Is. 11:7).

While we wait for the revealing of the sons of GOD, the forces that broke up the earth during the flood will continue to produce earthquakes and volcanoes.[33] This will be accompanied by a number of other significant natural catastrophes greater in scope than we have seen and which will also involve the natural heavens.[34]

Noah, in the line from Seth to Abraham and on to JESUS, was the keeper of a particular treasure. This treasure of his righteousness qualified him to be the keeper of the knowledge of GOD in his generation. He was particularly important in this role because he was the key survivor of the general flood that killed all the rest of humanity except his sons and all their wives. He was, then, the source of knowledge concerning GOD for the time to come. Whatever was deposited in him by his forebears was the content of the beliefs of mankind concerning GOD after the flood. This was a role GOD would not entrust to just anyone. When GOD acted to adjust The Creation, He made sure He had a qualified receptacle for truth – the man Noah. It seems reasonable that Noah would be particularly blessed in his spiritual capacities; that GOD would see to it that he possessed keen insight and wisdom concerning who GOD was. His life was the conduit through which the truth would be preserved.

In the next chapter, we'll consider how the knowledge of GOD would continue to be preserved in spite of the never-ending capacity of mankind for distorting or even forgetting it. The distortion of the knowledge of GOD is the source of all kinds of alternate "gods" who serve the purposes of men. It seems strange that GOD would entrust mere man with the truth of His nature, but that was His apparent plan from the beginning when He made Adam to be His viceroy.

---

[1] "Bloodline" refers to the specific biblical bloodline, whereas "race of Seth" refers to all mankind subsequent to the flood. The physical bloodlines were a shadow of the spiritual lineages from which our main lessons are to come.

[2] The physical mark of Cain occurred because of his precipitous spiritual fall to the status of murderer.

[3] Some readings of Exodus 19:1 interpret the arrival in the third month of the year, which would be exactly two months after leaving Egypt. Given the uncertainty in the text, it is still interesting that it was an exact time.

[4] Exodus 28:1-4 and Numbers 3:1-10 make clear that a very formal priesthood and Levitical function existed from that time onward.

[5] Exodus 19:10. Moses was to consecrate the people two days in a row. On the third day the "priests" were to consecrate themselves yet another time.

[6] This subject receives extensive treatment in chapter 8 of C. Gaulden, *Birth of The Holy Nation, Volume 1*, (Chambersburg, PA: eGen, 2015).

[7] It is probably true that the two of them interacted in this manner many times over the years. It is tempting to say he was one of the notables invited later to Isaac's weaning celebration at age five.

[8] It may be true that a better translation would be that they were "called BY the name of the Lord" rather than what we have. This would actually be consistent with the usage in Genesis 6.

[9] A guaranty is the substance of a guarantee. By this we mean that a guarantee is a promise and a guaranty is the collateral that validates the promise. In this case, Seth was a kind of continuation of Adam; his legacy. For us this means he would carry on the priesthood of Adam in his own generation and after the death of Adam should the death sequence occur as expected.

[10] Chapter 8 of Gaulden, *Birth of The Holy Nation, Volume 1*, explains who Melchizedek was.

[11] Genesis 5:22 suggests that Enoch enjoyed a very close relationship with GOD, which implies that the knowledge he received from his father was still accurate even after five generations. Furthermore, as a man in whom GOD delighted, Enoch might well have possessed unique knowledge.

[12] The Genesis 5 chronology indicates that Adam was 627 years old when Enoch was born and lived until Enoch was 303 years old. Adam, therefore, likely would have seen the high quality of Enoch's life and might well have been one of his main teachers of the knowledge of GOD. If so, he would certainly be pleased with how the fellow turned out.

[13] Again, this appears to have been a physical distinction, perhaps a distortion that produced what we might call Cro-Magnon or Neanderthal.

[14] Authorship of Genesis is ascribed to Moses, but the original material must have been written earlier. It is likely Moses received multiple documents that he compiled into Genesis as we know it.

[15] Perhaps Genesis 4:26 implies such a thing, at least for the bloodline.

[16] In the short passage (Gen. 6:1-8) it appears that the term "man" or "men" refers to the descendants of Cain. In order to distinguish the descendants of Seth from the descendants of Cain, a different word or term was needed. "Sons of God" was a device that could serve the purpose. Cainites displeased GOD in virtually every way. In particular, they encouraged Sethites to marry their daughters. This was the apex of their irritation of GOD. They brought genetic and cultural disorder into the families of the Sethites. It

was that to which His attention turned. I encourage you to read the passage and substitute Cainite for the word man or men throughout. This will clarify the matter. The text does not say the Nephilim were products of the intermarriages, only that they were around. They might well have been a result of the genetic chaos that accompanied the descendants of Cain. In blotting man from the face of the earth in this scenario, GOD was going to eradicate the direct descendants of Cain from the earth. While He was at it, He also eradicated most of the descendants of Seth. Perhaps the spiritual malaise they experienced came from their relationships with Cainites.

[17] When the memory of GOD is confused, other names and personalities for GOD emerge. New religions are a natural result of this kind of disorder.

[18] This might well have resulted in gigantism after the time of the flood. For example, Goliath (he was over nine feet tall according to 1 Sam. 17:4) might have been a manifestation of that genetic chaos. Scripture refers to other giants as well. See 2 Samuel 21:18-22 for a discussion.

[19] Shem's age at the time of the flood was 98. This is inferred from Genesis 11:10. Arpachshad was born two years after the flood when his father Shem was 100. Hence, the flood occurred when Shem was 98. Noah was 600 at the time of the flood (Gen. 7:6). So, he was 502 years when Shem was born. On the other hand, Noah was 500 years old when his first son was born (Gen. 6:32). This implies that one son of Noah was 2 years old when Shem was born. Furthermore, it is clear that Ham was the youngest son (Gen 9:24). Hence, the birth order was Japheth, Shem, and Ham. In Genesis 10:21 many translations read that Shem was the elder brother of Japheth, but a literal translation is that Shem was the brother of Japheth-the-elder.

[20] All the human, animal, and plant product of the chaos that accompanied Cain and his descendants was to be destroyed as well. This likely included such things as dinosaurs and so forth. Perhaps it is also true that predation came about in that chaotic environment and was passed on in some manner to animals that GOD sent to the ark. Noah did not gather animals for the ark; GOD sent them (Gen. 7:7-9). Therefore, it was GOD's business which animals He sent to Noah in the ark.

[21] The ark was a box. It was not a boat. Only something that could remain upright in the violent flooding that was to occur could have survived it.

[22] Genesis 6:20.

[23] As we noted in a previous endnote, evolution might well have been very chaotic in the environs of the descendants of Cain and all sorts of things might have come to be that would be "tidied up" in the flood. To some extent the chaos would continue after the flood but not to the same extent. This could have been the result, for example, of the passing on of genetic materials.

[24] Sam Soleyn has often taught on protection and provision. Abraham gave the name Jehovah Jireh (GOD is my provider) (Gen. 22:14). GOD promised to be a great shield to Abram (Gen. 15:1).

[25] Some propose that the climate of the earth was different because of a great cloud that prevailed before the flood. This proposition is also used to suggest where the great rains came from. The text does not give us that cloud cover. It is only inferred. The fountains of the great deep burst open, accompanied by a great rain. It might well be that the major portion of the water came from within the earth in the amazing tectonic fury that came about. It is true that rain had not previously fallen (Gen. 2:5-6) at the time of Adam's introduction into the garden. The text does not specify whether rain fell between then and the flood. The text does not resolve this matter.

[26] Inferred by comparing Genesis 7:11 and Genesis 8:4.

[27] This interpretation of a somewhat vague passage is probably controversial for some. The interpretation seems to fit the information provided. Genesis 8:7 is translated in various ways. One possible translation is that the raven flew "*back and forth*" rather than "*here and there*," for example.

[28] Genesis 8:21-22 implies this interpretation.

[29] Genesis 1:28 states that Adam was charged with ruling all other life on the earth. Genesis 9:2 states

that living animals would fear Noah. This is likely a feature of the change in diet. In Adam's time, they were told to eat plant matter. In Noah's time, meat was added to the menu. The instructions to Noah may also imply a simply more distant relationship between man and animal as a vestige of the chaos introduced by Cain into the world. Predator and prey relationships imply more distrust by their very nature.

[30] GOD instructed Noah concerning clean and unclean animals in terms of their presence on the ark (Gen. 7:2) without any information as to how the words were used. On the other hand, verses 8 and 9 reveal that the animals were sent. So, GOD simply imprinted into the minds of individual animals that they were to enter the ark. In some manner, though, Noah knew by the time of the sacrifice what it was he was to sacrifice. It might have been a simple matter of the numbers that informed Noah. We just don't know exactly how this occurred. The "clean" and "unclean" definitions were provided later under Aaronic regulations.

[31] This is not to suggest that GOD is petty. However, He seems to have been clear in His own mind about the distinction between clean and unclean. This is probably true even in The Eternal.

[32] Mankind and the rest of the earth component of The Creation are in a continuous state of decline until the sons of GOD are revealed. Man is not ascending, but descending. He is less capable, not more capable. It is true that technology is used to substitute for capability. It is not true that technology makes us more personally capable. In fact, technology produces elites rather than assuming all are personally capable. For example, we are no longer aware of how the Egyptians produced the pyramids. There are many ideas, but we cannot prove we are as smart and as capable as they were.

[33] Revelation 6:12 speaks of a very significant earthquake that will occur at the opening of the sixth seal. This will likely be the greatest earthquake since the flood. It will, in a sense, mark a paroxysm of frustration of the earth a little while before the revelation of the sons of GOD. This time of tumult will be so great that leaders of men will hide themselves and prefer suicide over remaining in the earth (Rev. 6:14-17).

[34] I find three heavens: physical space and two supernatural realms. For a discussion, see chapter two above.

CHAPTER NINE

NOAH AND DESCENDANTS

In the previous chapter we examined some matters related to the flood occasioned by GOD's displeasure with the way "sons of God" were dishonoring Him. This specifically occurred in the matter of marriages of the **sons of GOD** with daughters of the **race of Cain**. The humanist might rail at GOD and call Him unfair in this matter, but He was interested in accurate representation of His person in the earth and such marriages could only compromise such a representation. In order to restore the representation, He found a righteous man to carry forward the knowledge of who He was. That man was Noah. He also saw to it that some land-based animals and flying creatures survived the flood in the company of the righteous man. He then obliterated that which had become so perverse.

When GOD saved Noah to carry on His legacy, so to speak, He also kept Noah's family safe with him so that the legacy would be able to move forward with the history of mankind. These three sons and the wives of the four men were the only human survivors (1 Pe. 3:20). It would be Noah's responsibility to carry forward the spiritual aspects of that legacy. It would be the lot of the three sons to begin the repopulation of the earth. This is where we find ourselves at this point.

One People

It goes without saying that when Noah's family came out of the ark, there was but one culture in the world. All other cultures and subcultures had been eliminated in the flood. The keeper and source of authority for the one culture now found in the world was Noah. Surely his wife had memories of the past before the flood, as did his sons and their wives, but the source of authority, identity, and culture was Noah.

Let's consider that for a moment. There were no real differences of practice or observance in matters of life or of spiritual concern. There were no other cultural behaviors. There was only the one way of living–Noah's way. There was only one language. There was only one creation narrative. There was only one way of doing virtually everything. That way was *the way of Noah*. There was only one authoritative knowledge of GOD in the whole world. To the extent that Noah accurately represented GOD to his family, that family had an accurate concept and knowledge of GOD (see Gen. 11:1) to go forward with. As there was only one family, GOD would be well represented and remembered because He had found the requisite quality in Noah.

We know that about two years after the flood–one year out of the ark–Shem produced his first son. Soon, all three of Noah's sons were producing children. Scripture credits Japheth with seven sons, Ham with four, and Shem with five (Gen. 10:1-22). Logically, these sons would be very important persons in time. In fact, as we shall see, the first "ethnicities" of men bore their names. By this we mean that Noah's sons' sons would eventually become the fathers of peoples called by their own names. So the sons of Canaan, for example would be called Canaanites, but there would be several varieties of Cannanites, including Hittites, for example. If the scriptural list is complete, there were sixteen grandsons in Noah's house. That is quite a start for repopulating the earth. As was the case in the time of Seth, it is necessary for us to accept that these grandsons would marry their close kinswomen; first cousins being the most distant in the first post-flood generation. At that time, there were no other people present in the earth from among whom women could be found to marry Noah's grandsons.

Sons and daughters began to be born to Noah's sons, and as the children reached appropriate ages, they married and began to produce yet another generation. And so it was. Noah's three sons had sixteen listed sons among them. From the one man in Noah's generation who had survived the flood, there were 20 men and an undisclosed number of women in a fairly short period of time after the flood. If we assume a ratio of about one female child to one male child in the third and subsequent generations, and if we assume an average of five sons to be born to each male, a very sizeable population would come about in several decades. It is worth noting that the lifespans of the generations after the flood fell off quickly thereafter.[1] At the same time, we note that the age at which the "key son" was born to each succeeding generation began to fall off very quickly as well.[2] For example, Shem was 100 years old when his son Arpachshad was born to him. On the other hand, Arpachshad was only 35 years old when Shelah was born to him, and so forth.[3]

Throughout this period of rapid expansion in the size of the human population of the earth, *the single culture of Noah* continued to prevail. The growth in the size of the population did not yet cause the people to lose contact with one another. As long as Noah remained alive, his personal presence among the people continued to be important to them. This was the man who had been warned by GOD concerning the great flood. He would certainly make sure his descendants (every living human was one) knew the story quite well. His human heart probably believed that this would keep the people from returning to the wickedness that had led to the flood to begin with. He was also a righteous man, the most righteous in his generation (Gen. 6:9). As such, he would be motivated to pass along the knowledge of GOD to his descendants as long as he lived among the people. Thus, as long as the descendants of Noah stayed where Noah was, they had the best knowledge of GOD that was available in the earth. Only when any one of them decided to turn away from that truth would there begin to be corruption in their "doctrine."

The First "Division"

Alas, it seems to be true that human nature (the soul) will develop a flaw if it can. After Noah and his sons left the ark, the sons began the repopulation process. In some number of years–probably not many–the full tally of 16 sons had been born. As those sons grew toward the time of their natural maturity, a fairly tight-knit family went about the processes of life. Noah continued to teach them and to offer up sacrifices to God, which we can be sure they were invited to as witnesses. He trained them in the ways of the Lord as he knew them.

Noah also became a farmer. Obviously, food was a primary concern among them. They had become omnivores after leaving the ark (compare Gen. 1:29-30 to Gen. 9:3-4). This required that some effort also be put into raising food animals. Abel had raised animals, which we may infer were not eaten but were used for other things like milk. Now animals were also to be sources of food for Noah's descendants.[4]

Among Noah's farming ventures was a vineyard. We all know the story. On one occasion, Noah became drunk on wine made from the produce of his vineyard. The narrative does not suggest this was a regular occurrence. In fact, it only records this one occurrence. For whatever reason, when Noah went in to "sleep it off," he did so only after disrobing. Sometime later Ham (who knows why?) went into Noah's tent and found his father in his disrobed status.[5] Something in Ham's nature led him to despise what his father had done. In so doing, he despised his father. There is no evidence of any previous rift between the two of them, but now Ham despised his father. As a result, he ridiculed his father to his brothers soon afterward.

This produced a fracture in the family. Ham's ridicule of his father grew to where he was unable to respect his father. Once that condition began to set in, family harmony was harmed. In this scenario it is easy to imagine Ham questioning any dictum from Noah and challenging his father's authority outright. Under those conditions, maintaining family harmony was impossible.

It is interesting that Ham tried immediately to "teach" his brothers some measure of disrespect for their father. They each then had to decide how to react. If they too began to disrespect Noah, they too would begin to question him frequently. This would introduce utter chaos into the family. To be fair to Ham, we cannot assume he knew what these dynamics would look like. He was only following his self-directed feelings. We, on the other hand, can learn from these events.

Shem and Japheth maintained proper respect for their father. They did not respond in kind to Ham's ridicule of him. They decided instead to continue to respect their father and to return him to a more respectable state. They would not look on their father's nakedness and thus dishonor him. They decided to keep the culture intact along with the principle of respect for their father.[6] In so doing, they preserved the value of the primacy of their father. Whether they thought it out or not, they were honoring divine, godly order in their actions. By physically covering the nakedness of their father, they symbolically restored the order of the family. That they did so in the manner they selected lifted what they did above all reproach, in stark contrast to the wickedness of their brother Ham.[7] They risked a feud with their brother for the sake of something on a higher order. In so doing, they insured at least partial continuity of the culture of GOD in the earth. Further, they represented the truth that father-son relationships are of greater import than brother-brother relationships.

And then Noah had a problem. Fortunately, Shem and Japheth had supported and preserved his dignity, which would insure the continuity of the family. However, the dishonor shown by Ham was a matter that needed remedy. It could not simply be ignored. The entire population of the earth would soon know of the matter. That could not be avoided. These events probably happened within 30-50 years after the flood while the population was still quite small (maybe less than 250 persons) and not dispersed to any degree. In other words, this was about like a village at the time. Whether Ham intended it or not, he had challenged his father's leadership, and, in that setting, the challenge had to be answered.[8] It could not be ignored. If the relationship between Noah and Ham was permanently ruptured, Ham would be a veritable orphan and a whole new kind of culture would emerge in the earth, the culture of the orphan. An orphan culture denigrates the father principle. In so doing, it diminishes the perceived authority of the Father. In turn, chaos is the likely outcome.

At the same time, Ham had been on the ark with Noah. That was surely an important fact in the community. In time, he would be one of the keepers of that memory. To exile Ham would make no sense as this would set up a potentially hostile relationship in the very small population, and make two populations with some degree of stress between them, as was probably the case between Cain and Seth and their families.

Noah's solution was an interesting one. He chose to have the youngest son of Ham bear the result of the guilt of his father. This son was likely to have the least salient relationship with his father or his grandfather. He was furthest in time from the flood, at least among the descendants of Ham. Ham and the three older brothers of Canaan would not bear that guilt and responsibility. In a sense, this removed the problem from the center of the community. At the same time, Ham and his other sons would know that disrespect for Noah brought no good result. Surely Noah hoped this would end the breach caused by Ham's disrespect for him. Noah and his drunkenness did not cause the breach; Ham did with his disrespect.

We don't know how old Canaan, Ham's youngest son, was at the time of his sentencing by Noah. It seems fair to assume he was a grown man and that the "sentence" began immediately. There were three key operational components to the curse or sentence of Canaan. First, he would not find refuge in the home of his father Ham. He was to be a lowly servant to even his own brothers: Cush, Mizraim, and Put. Canaan was specifically assigned to his uncle Shem as a servant and, secondarily, to his uncle Japheth. In essence, Canaan would have no one in the earth to protect him. It was as though he had become an orphan with no family at all. In this state he would receive no estate from his father and would always be at the mercy of others. It is not likely that he was actually mistreated by his kinsmen. Rather, he lost his place among them. He had no rights and would live as they determined, not as he determined.[9]

Ham's contempt for his father created a permanent *division* within the family of Noah, a division that isolated the principle of paternal

182

respect from the orphan's mindset. In essence, Canaan was subjected to a sort of internal exile. This was to play out in the subsequent history of the Shemites and Canaanites because of the location of the Canaanites after the dispersion that came a bit later in the history of mankind. At the end of the matter, in fact, the Canaanites settled (after the dispersion) in a location that was a kind of meeting of all three branches of Noah's family (Japheth, Shem and Ham).

The Great Division

It seems the families of Noah's sons remained essentially intact even after the curse on Canaan. The tenth chapter of Genesis presents a fairly comprehensive listing of the generations of Noah's grandsons and great-grandsons. There were sixteen grandsons. Some 70 persons are listed in the fourth and fifth generations, in addition to the 20 men in the first three generations, including Noah. Obviously, repopulation was well under way.

Genesis 10:25 presents us with an interesting observation. The fellow named Eber (son of Shelah, son of Arpachshad, son of Shem, son of Noah,) in the fifth generation starting from Noah, had a son he named Peleg, which means "division."[10] It seems quite reasonable to propose that the division referred to in the naming of this son was the political and geographic division of the peoples after the attempt to reach heaven at Babel. Counting from Noah, Peleg was in the sixth generation after the flood. Thus, if Eber was there at the time of the division, then the division took place when the fifth generation was becoming the reproducing generation. Hence, Peleg in the sixth generation was named after the division.

Another interesting aspect of the tenth chapter of Genesis is that the chapter transcends the story of Babel and its tower (which is found in Gen. 11). That is, the time in which the tower of Babel incident took place was the same time when Eber was producing sons (see Gen. 10:25). If we converted Genesis 11:1-9 into a footnote, we could attach it to Genesis 10:25 as explaining the naming of Peleg.

If these conclusions are accurate, we may have an explanation for the fellow Nimrod, who was a grandson of Ham through Cush (Gen. 10:8-12). The detail presented on the life of Nimrod seems fairly disconnected otherwise. It is likely that most of his exploits occurred after the tower of Babel events. His position in the fourth generation makes this at least feasible. One may infer, but not prove, a kind of pugnacity in Nimrod that makes him stand out in the narrative. Note that Nimrod was not a descendant of Canaan, but a nephew. Also note that Nimrod *founded* Babel, or was at least instrumental in its establishment. It was probably later that he founded other cities further east.

We can think of Genesis 10 as a useful introduction to the peoples of the earth who were descended from Noah. They all lived together and spoke the same language for quite a while (Gen. 11:1-4).[11] Their reasoning in the decision to build the tower in Babel is quite interesting. They built the tower to keep themselves together. If they felt the need to remain together, they must have been under some pressure to separate. In other words, some of their "leaders" were concerned that social forces among them threatened to force them into small groups.[12] The tower of Babel, they hoped, would provide a focal point of activity that would keep the people together.

Thus, the people in the fourth and fifth generations felt a strong desire to find a way to remain together. This seems to run counter to the command the Lord had given to Noah (Gen. 9:7). The narrative implies that GOD wanted the people to cover the whole face of the earth and exhibit His presence everywhere. If they remained together they would not soon be found all over the earth.[13]

It was GOD Himself, then, who confounded their purpose. They purposed to band themselves together at a place called Babel. If they did that, they would not fill the earth. Hence, their purpose at Babel was inconsistent with GOD's purpose. His intervention was needed to cause them to split apart from one another in the earth to populate the whole earth and represent GOD there. While the purpose of the people would not have been the purpose of Noah, it was the purpose of at least a large proportion of the people. Their intent at Babel was a matter of pride (and maybe fear) that stood in the way of GOD's will.

184

GOD acted to disrupt their ability to communicate. Very quickly, the people found themselves speaking many languages rather than the one they had previously shared. The narrative implies this was basically instantaneous. It appears this happened to families rather than individuals and followed the lines of kinship outlined in Genesis 10. In other words, one day the folks went to work and members of any given family could no longer understand the folks from other families. Some languages were fairly similar. For example, the Javanites and Tubalites could probably understand each other reasonably well (Gen. 10:2). But the Javanites and the Amorites couldn't communicate very well at all. Closer kinship seems to have meant more similarity in the new languages.[14] More distance in kinship seems to have resulted in very little similarity. This new phenomenon must have been frightening. Yesterday, everyone could understand everyone. Today, something had happened to nearly *everybody else*, and efforts to coordinate the great work of the tower in Babel fell apart. Without a common language, it could no longer be pursued. The frustration of not being able to communicate probably also bred immediate suspicion of the motives of others who could not be understood. Soon, cautious suspicion began to lead the various families and family groups to wander away from one another. Eventually, this migration spread the people out in every direction until people were present in all hospitable regions.

This method of division was not necessary originally. Had Noah and his sons begun to move more freely in the earth, they might well have met GOD's mandate without this time of great confusion.[15] But they did not do so. Imagine Noah's pain as his descendants began to not trust one another. No doubt, some forces of disagreement had always been among them. Suddenly, though, they were practically flying apart. Noah's sons might not have even been able to understand him any longer. Or, perhaps, Shem could understand Noah but Japheth and Ham (and their descendants) could not. Now, people speaking many different languages began to migrate to different locations with their nearest kin and away from their more distant kin.[16]

For example, Mizraim (son of Ham) and his descendants began a migration that ended in the northeastern-most part of Africa. This area came to be known by his name (Mizraim means Egypt in Hebrew). Initially, they would have traveled with the other descendants of Ham: Cush, Put, and Canaan.[17] In time, Noah's grandsons and later descendants would give their names to various parts of the earth. Some of those names (e.g. Mizraim) and their derivatives remain with us even today.[18]

Genesis 11:7 specifically attributes the confounding of speech as a deliberate act on GOD's part to cause the people to scatter and to move to all parts of the earth. This was a purpose, not a blind consequence. It seems likely that the migrations began immediately after the speech confusion began. It also seems likely that the various groups moved in such a way as to avoid one another. The various groups that were descended from Ham moved mostly to the south and west into what is now Africa. The groups that were descended from Japheth moved mostly northward, some more easterly and some more westerly. The groups that were descended from Shem did not really wander very far. They seem to have remained centered not too far from Babel. These are very broad generalizations, of course. We know, for example, that Nimrod, who was descended from Ham by way of Cush, actually seems to have moved in the opposite direction to the other Cushites (northeast rather than southwest). In any event, the various family groups (ethnicities, if you will) moved away from one another in such a way as to minimize frictions among them, at least initially. This process might have been fairly rapid at the beginning, only to slow down as the groups felt that "safe" distances had been achieved. Also, as the groups grew larger, pace of migration naturally would slow down.

Canaanites

One group of particular interest to us is the Canaanites. They moved generally south and west with the other Hamites, but did not go as far south. They moved into an area north and east of the Miz-raimites (Egyptians), and the various tribes of them (e.g. Amorites and Hivites) settled in an area that came to be known as Canaan because that is where they were. They were not among the rest of the Hamites, but were adjacent to them. This destination also placed them just west of the Shemites, some of whom went in that same direction but not so far. In short, the Canaanites were separated from the early western Shemites (now called Semites) only by a frontier formed by the Jordan River. The lands to the east of the river were occupied by some of the Semitic groups. This, in essence, placed the Canaanites between the other Hamites and the Semites. Just up the coast to the north were the southernmost of the Japhethite peoples.

An interesting feature of the movements of the Canaanites was their condition of servitude, to Shem in particular. It might be that their final destination was determined by Shem himself. He was definitely still alive at the time. Perhaps he even lived among them (at least part of the time) in order to take advantage of their servitude to him and of their default dependence on him as their master. Wherever they would live, other peoples could contest their being there. However, if Shem were present, he would offer them a kind of legitimacy.

At the same time, Shem's descendants seem to have remained near the original homeland, which was nearer to Babel.[19] These events seem to have happened well over two hundred years before the death of Noah. It appears the Shemites remained near him and the other peoples moved away from him. Out of deference to him, it is quite likely that his decision to remain more or less where he was at the time of Babel was honored by nearly all the people, and his location determined the place from which the migrations would be taken. It would be very difficult to make an argument that Shem was not regarded as the next man after Noah to represent GOD.

In addition, there is no reason to believe that war was a feature of these early movements, at least not typically.[20] Rather, it seems the migrations helped prevent dangerous tensions for quite a while. War came later when groups of men began to wander forth from secondary centers of settlement in various directions in search of their own locations as newly emerging ethnicities continued to split off from main groups over time.[21]

Religious Orientation

At the time of the big division at Babel, there was only one culture, as we have already seen. On the other hand, there were forces at work among the people that eventually led to cultural troubles. The confusion of the languages forced the people apart along "fault lines" that already existed between the various families. For example, Ham's contempt for his father and Noah's subsequent cursing of Canaan must have created tensions between Ham and his sons in their relations with the families of Shem and Japheth.[22] Such tensions were managed fairly well as long as Noah was with the people. After the Babel events, however, Noah was no longer among the Hamites and the Japhethites as they moved away from the area. In the case of Ham and his descendants, their natural animosities soon began to bring about new interpretations of their history as a people and diminish the stature of Noah. In that environment, they soon began to "reinterpret" GOD also.

Ham and his sons took what Noah had taught them about GOD and changed it and added to that knowledge so that before long their beliefs and practices diverged significantly from those that Noah and Shem kept constant. These new beliefs took on even more importance over time as the life conditions of the families simply were no longer like those of their distant kinsmen. In a few generations, they even ceased to remember there ever was a Noah or what he believed. Their new beliefs, which arose in conjunction and accord with their location and experiences, gradually overcame any residuals of Noah's influence. Those who encountered these people later in history found that their religious beliefs and practices were quite different from those of other groups.

In time, linguistic and religious differences would so isolate the psyches of the various groups that leaders could exploit their different awarenesses for their own purposes. In turn, men would now become isolated from one another in virtually all their attitudes and would become fully competitive in the earth. As populations increased and power became centralized, the competition for resources would also increase as men found it harder and harder to move to new places. Tensions would lead to efforts by leaders to focus the will of the people on their own identity and to denigrate the cultures of other people. In very general terms, that is how we got from Babel to the here-and-now.

In such environments, political leaders find it expedient to manipulate the religious sensitivities of people in order to control them. This natural tendency is demonstrated, for example, in the story of Joseph and the Egyptians.[23] In a sense, the political and religious sensitivities of a people can both become subservient to the needs of the state, further separating peoples from a common understanding of who GOD is.

The "Priesthood"

Without Noah around, it was unreasonable to expect the various groups to maintain a very authentic awareness of GOD. On the other hand, GOD would always keep a man who could maintain that awareness, regardless of what others did. Noah had been such a man. Shem was to be such a man. As this line was true to an accurate portrayal of GOD, so GOD would have a man in each generation to make that possible. Shem would pass on to Arpachshad an accurate memory. Arpachshad would pass that on to Shelah , who would pass it on to Eber. Eber would pass that on to Peleg, and so forth.[24] So even at the time of failure at Babel, the accurate presentation of GOD remained. In time, that knowledge would be found in a Shemite named Abram. He would become the father of a nation designated by GOD to be a whole people who could remember and represent GOD accurately in the earth.[25]

The other two main branches of mankind in this era (Hamites and Japhethites) were not included in this *de facto* "priesthood" of GOD. The religions that developed among their descendants were kept by their own priesthoods. These priesthoods were, however, in the hands of men who had not had access to an accurate knowledge of GOD. Their ideas of who GOD was became less and less accurate over time. GOD, however, would have a people who could accurately and adequately represent Him in the earth. This was a key component of the redemptive plan–that all men would one day see the correct representation of GOD in the sons of GOD who had descended from those who knew Him at the beginning. We know this as a spiritual phenomenon, but it was represented in the identities of various men in these very early times.

The main line of this priesthood runs from Adam to JESUS through Noah and Shem and on to Abram. The chart below captures this line from the time of the flood to the appearance of Abram. It was Abram to whom was given the task of converting a man into the nation of GOD's choosing.

BIRTH YEAR (FROM CREATION)	THE "PRIEST"	LIFESPAN	DEATH YEAR
1061	Noah	950	2011
1561	Japheth (info only)		
1563	Shem	600	2163
1661	**THE FLOOD**		
1663	Arpachshad	438	2101
1698	Shelah	433	2131
1728	Eber	464	2192
?	**BABEL TOWER**		
1762	Peleg	239	2001
1792	Reu	239	2031
1824	Serug	230	2054
1854	Nahor	148	2002
1883	Terah	205	2088
2013	Abram/Abraham	175	2188

These men are listed in the post-flood narrative as the one man in each generation who best kept the knowledge of GOD. They are also found in the direct ancestry of JESUS (Lk. 3:34-38).

A specific contrivance appears in the table. The birth of Abram is set to cause his immigration to Canaan to fit at the time of the death of his father Terah.[26] If this assertion is correct, then Abram arrived in Canaan 2088 years after the creation. That being the case (if it is), Shem, Arpachshad, Shelah, and Eber were still alive. Shem was likely to be in Canaan with the various Canaanite peoples.[27] The three generations right after him would still be in the east in the Shemite lands, or possibly one or all of them were with Shem. The latter is not likely the case. All the ramifications of these things are simply beyond the scope of this work, however interesting they might be.

Our argument is that Abram was a kind of priest, having received a full education in the knowledge of GOD from Shem, and the fathers after him, as they had received it from Noah. When Abram went to Canaan, he was the man in his generation who had the most accurate sense of who GOD was. This means that his brother back in *Aram Nahoraim* was to pass on less accurate information to his descendants. In that way, GOD had the man of His choosing in the land of His choosing by the time Abram arrived in Canaan. This was to be the specific mechanism for passing on into history the true knowledge of GOD.

---

[1] Some propose that the falloff in age is a function of the loss of the hypothetical cloud that persisted before the flood. That cloud's loss would produce a harsher climate that could be the reason for earlier mortality. Some interpret Genesis 6:6 as a prediction of diminishing lifespan. That appears to be more about the time remaining before the flood, but the alternate is suggested by some. If that be so, it took quite some time for human lifespan to diminish to the 120-year point. We must remember that genetic change is generally in the negative direction insofar as life and health are concerned. The cumulative genetic changes from the time before the flood may be the reason. We are only recently witnessing increases in average lifespan, but that seems to be more a product of medical technology than of integrity of genetic material. Whatever the reason, lifespan began to diminish soon after the flood.

[2] That is the general case, but Abram was not born at an early age for Terah. I argue Terah was about 130 years old when Abram was born as his *youngest* son. This is inferred from the fact that Abram was 75 years old when he migrated. GOD would not take him from his father Terah, so He waited for Abram to become a natural "orphan" He could adopt at 75 years of age. The argument related to birth order is the same as the one forwarded for Shem; the prominent son is listed first (Gen. 11:27) rather than the firstborn.

[3] This trend of younger fathers persisted until Terah, the father of Abram, who began to produce sons at age 70. This may be explained by the need to fit in the "generating" generations before Abram and making room for most of them to die (except Shem and Eber) before Abram emerged.

[4] The Cainites might have been using animals for food before the flood. Remember, they were quite dissimilar to the Sethites.

[5] The narrative does not say anything else about Noah's condition when Ham saw him. Some propose he was having sexual relations with his wife when Ham entered. That seems unlikely based on the clear meaning of the text and that his other sons found him in the same condition sometime later.

[6] This is a very important fundamental. Respect for His Father is a hallmark of the life of JESUS. The primacy of a father is the paramount property of human relations.

[7] Their averted faces resisted even the temptation to dishonor their father even though he was in a compromised situation.

[8] Had Noah not taken the matter seriously and sought remedy, his primacy would have been permanently challenged. This would soon give rise to democracy, which devalues primacy until it no longer matters. The destruction of the people would soon follow. This is not a political statement; it is a spiritual observation. It was not GOD's intent that the people rule themselves; they were to respect primacy for their survival. That was at least true for that time. Later, democracy would begin to prevail (even before Noah's death) and would result in the tower in Babel.

[9] On the other hand, if Canaan and his family lived an isolated life without supervision by Shem, he could pretty much do as he wished. He was not necessarily mistreated but lost any right to appeal if he were mistreated. He could not own land as he could not receive an estate. This was to be a perpetual condition of his offspring as well because there was no one from whom his descendants could inherit an estate.

[10] Peleg (Strong's, 6389) seems to mean "earthquake" and comes from a root meaning "to divide." It might mean a tectonic storm, but that seems unlikely because he was born long after the flood. Rather, it is likely he was born soon after the division of the peoples by ethnicity at the time of the tower in Babel.

[11] If the ages of the various generational fathers at the time of birth of the main sons is used as a guide, it appears to have been around 150 years after the flood to the tower in Babel.

[12] However, GOD had told them to "populate the earth abundantly and multiply in it" (Gen. 9:7). This would necessitate their scattering throughout the earth. They could not fulfill GOD's mandate if they remained together. In fact, we know that crowded humans go to war.

[13] There is no reason to believe there was more than one continent before the flood. Now there were several. Remaining together just would not get the job done. After all, it is His purpose that men represent Him in all the earth. These continents needed human inhabitants.

[14] For this reason, the descendants of the various sons of Canaan ended up in a land that came to be called Canaan. It was theirs in trust only because Canaan and his descendants could not legitimately own land in the eyes of GOD.

[15] I propose that Noah and Shem did not move a great distance from where the ark landed in the mountains of what is now the nation of Turkey. Their descendants down to the time of Abram had no reason to move. As the confounding of languages distanced the various peoples from Noah, they began to leave him. He would not have been driven to migrate. Most teach that the place called Ur of the Chaldees was in the lower Tigris-Euphrates valley. There is an Ur in that area and it was occupied by the Chaldees. However, they originated in the mountain country near Ararat. They arrived late in Ur. I contend it is not necessary to call the city Ur of the Chaldees unless there is more than one city named Ur. The Chaldees probably began their relocation after Abram left home with his father Terah. I propose that

the name of the place implies a location near to the ark landing place and the likely place where Noah finished out his life. This place was north of Shinar. Such a scenario makes the migrations of Terah and Abram more reasonable.

[16] Jewish legend has it that 70 ethnicities were involved. It is probably true that nearly everyone who came after Noah was still alive at the time of the tower. There were about 70 of those named in the first three generations. They were then the name-fathers of the various migrating groups.

[17] Canaan might have been restricted somewhat in his migrations by Shem, as Shem had that right. Both Shem and Canaan would still be alive. We can verify that Shem was by his lifespan. Canaan was more than 100 years younger than Shem and the tower debacle happened only about 150 years after the flood.

[18] Some modern scholars argue that this is just an artifact of a biblical mindset on the part of early ethnographers. That argument, however, could easily prove to be spurious and is likely to simply be a product of mindsets who do not want it to be true that people possessed these identities. In other words, some scholars don't want the Bible to be true, so they propose the names are artificial.

[19] Refer to the previous note explaining the likely northern location of Ur of the Chaldees.

[20] Once the ethnicities had settled into their new geographic locations, war would soon emerge as boundaries began to be "negotiated." This would definitely be true as new ethnicities emerged or land became relatively scarcer due to population growth. Land and other wealth were primary causes of war until fairly modern times and really still are.

[21] "New" ethnicities are a constant phenomenon and are typically both a result and a cause of strife. One family within an ethnic would grow to significant size and begin to be aggrieved at how the rest of their neighbors treated them. As groups grow, they begin to look for power for themselves. They will also begin to differentiate themselves from their "neighbors" and seek some sort of separation for themselves in the name of charting their own destiny.

[22] There is no reasonable doubt that GOD ratified that curse after Noah announced it. For that reason, the displacement of the Canaanites from Canaan several hundred years later did not violate GOD's sense of justice.

[23] When Joseph was elevated to the high position he occupied in Egypt, he received a new (Egyptian) name and an Egyptian wife. She was the daughter of a prominent Egyptian priest (Gen. 41:45). Some ten years later, Joseph excused the priest class in Egypt from economic debasement during the lean years. In fact, he saw to it that they were on the royal payroll, kept their property, and did not have to pay taxes to Pharaoh (Gen. 47:22). This is similar to the Edict of Toleration issued by the Roman Emperor in the fourth century.

[24] Written records were surely being kept by then. GOD would have seen to that. These men, each in his generation, might even have been stewards of those written records, being sure they were passed down. Those records would eventually find their way to Egypt, to be hidden there until the exodus occurred. At that time, they were likely turned over to Moses for his work and their preservation.

[25] It is likely that Abram received the records at the time of the death of his father Terah. In Chapter 8 of C. Gaulden, *Birth of The Holy Nation, Volume 1*, (Chambersburg, PA: eGen, 2015) I discuss this as a component of the relationship between Abram and Melchizedek.

[26] First, GOD honors fatherhood and would not violate that of Terah. Only after Terah was gone would He "adopt" Abram. Second, the conditions GOD placed on Abram made him an orphan needing adoption (Gen. 12:1). He was to leave his family and his inheritance to follow GOD. This made him a *de facto* orphan.

[27] Chapter 8 of *Birth of The Holy Nation, Volume 1*, explains who Melchizedek almost surely was.

CHAPTER TEN

CONCLUSIONS

GOD created the earth and the rest of what we call The Creation with a purpose in mind. We know that He *knows the end from the beginning.*[1] While that is true, it is also true that He *created the beginning from the end.* He never wavered or doubted in His purpose. In the earliest chapters of the book of Genesis, we can see how He began the process that leads to "a kingdom and priests to our God" who will "reign upon the earth" (Rev. 5:10). He began by creating a man to "reign upon the earth." The reign of GOD is a perfect reign. The man failed his promise. GOD had created the man to be "reign-ready." That means that the man was fully capable, and he was "perfect" until he decided not to maintain the behavioral likeness of GOD.[2] When that occurred, GOD set in motion a plan of redemption that would lead to "a kingdom and priests to our God" to "reign upon the earth." He will have His way in the matter. That "kingdom" is the manifestation of GOD's intention in the creation of the man. The end determined what the beginning would be like.

In fact, we have deliberately used the passage in Revelation to set the tone and context for this analysis of the book of "beginnings." When we view the beginning from the point of view of the end, we can effectively integrate the entire biblical narrative. Our historical tendency is to see biblical texts as a group of stories gathered into various types rather than as a work with only one key point. That key point is that GOD intends for a reliable and accurate representation of Himself to be seen in the being of something called "a kingdom and priests." He designed the entire creation around that intent.

Men have had many different opinions about the identity and character of GOD, and still do. For the most part, the various ideas are a mixture of truth and self-serving purposes. Some are simply perversions based on disappointments. Others are deliberate distortions designed to serve some political goal. GOD, in His own interests, would have to see to it that mankind had access to accurate portrayals of Him. In order to do that, He needed to insert Himself into the saga of humanity on an ongoing basis. Every human being interprets GOD however he will. The longer GOD remains distant from any particular interpretation, the more inaccurate it will become. GOD's solution to the "wandering concept" of who He is has been to choose representatives and to do so in such a way that He is always represented fairly accurately.

First Natural Sons

The first human son of GOD had all the information he needed to accurately and adequately represent GOD in the earth. He failed because his own interests interfered with what he knew to be true. Adam did not intend to not represent GOD. Even in the best of his intentions, though, he failed. Into his hands then fell the task of keeping alive the memory of what had been at the very first. His sons had only his word for that. They had not been present when the fall occurred. To some extent, Adam's failings would color his perceptions, but GOD would correct that deficiency as He saw fit.

Then Seth would have the history of Cain and Abel in his awareness. By the time the history of mankind had come down to Noah over sixteen centuries later, a lot of distortion could have occurred. Had GOD just allowed all the humans in those years to rely on their own ideas about Him, there would have been no righteous man found in the earth. GOD, being no fool, selected out in every generation a man with whom He would have closer fellowship than with other

196

men in that generation. For example, Abel knew the ways of GOD more accurately than did his brother Cain, even though Cain was the older of the two. Abel's removal through his murder at the hands of his brother Cain necessitated that another (Seth) be born to be the one "closer" to GOD.

Among the sons of Seth was a man named Enosh. We do not know his birth order. What we know is that he was the man in his generation closest to GOD. Enosh had sons and daughters. Among them was a man named Kenan (Cainan). His birth order is uncertain, but he was the man in his generation who was closest to GOD. We cannot say how these men maintained their relationships with GOD, but they seem to be the ones in whom truth met its best match. GOD included each of them in his time in a close relationship that preserved for the future generations an accurate and adequate memory of who GOD was. We saw earlier that we can think of these guys as a kind of senior priesthood to keep the representation focused.

We can be sure that each of them "messed it up" in his own way, but we can also be sure GOD saw to it that the truth was ongoing.[3] When the time of the generation of Noah had come, Noah was that man. In that he "found favor in the eyes of the Lord" (Gen. 6:8), he was the man in his generation who had the most accurate representation of GOD and who could be trusted to keep it for the generations after the flood. It is likely that Noah also had with him whatever written records had begun to accumulate. That would be a "priestly" function.

The Priests

If we designate Adam (through Seth) as one end of a continuum, and Noah as the other, this bloodline was the one that made it possible for men to right themselves from time to time. The descendants of Seth, as specified in the fifth chapter of Genesis, were the men who connect these two points in history: the creation and the flood. GOD was never fully lost to men in that timeframe and the fellows in the direct bloodline bore the responsibility that it be so. Even though all other men, Cainites and Sethites, had turned away from GOD, when the time came Noah was in place to fulfill that responsibility.

After the flood GOD continued with the same program. In each generation, a particular man stood out as the conservator of the knowledge of GOD for his generation. All men in each generation had access to redemption, but GOD chose one to carry the message forward in each generation. That way He insured that the truth would never be unknown in the earth.[4]

So the purpose of GOD was to have sons in the earth so that The Creation could see its Creator in the person of a man who would bear the image and likeness of GOD. Behind that motivation was a love motivation: the love of the Father for the Son. This powerful force was to be extended to the entirety of The Creation through the man. The man would need to choose to be fully a son of GOD. For that reason, GOD built a redemptive mechanism into His plans.

The Stage

To get this whole thing underway, GOD would produce the context within which it would be enacted and played out. That context was The Creation itself with an emphasis on the earth, which would now depend on the quality of the man who was put into it to be the viceroy of GOD–a son of GOD.

From our perspective from within The Creation, the bringing forth of The Creation was an amazing phenomenon. The Creation included not only the earth but also other macro-phenomena we call "the heavens." During the process of creation, He also created three "heavens" to accompany the earth for a variety of purposes. The earth came with an atmosphere necessary to sustain life and to preserve water for life. The first heaven (First Heaven) contained what we call "heavenly bodies" that help govern cycles of life in the earth. A third heaven (Third Heaven) contained all else that was necessary to keep The Creation successfully suspended in The Eternal. An intermediate heaven (Second Heaven) has become the temporary dwelling place for the accuser and for all spiritual entities that position themselves against GOD and Man.

The acts of creation culminated in the preparation of the specific, proximal home of the viceroy. This specific address, if you will, was particularly suited to the needs of the viceroy and to the purposes of GOD. He, in essence, constructed a temple in which the man would dwell. The temple consisted of a "holy place" called Eden and a "most holy place" called the garden. In the most holy place, GOD placed the *tree of life*.[5] I believe this *tree of life* was present in the garden in Eden and in Third Heaven simultaneously. In some sense, its co-location in the two places was the extension of the infinite into the finite.[6] It was the center of spiritual power in the natural world at the time The Creation was finished. This was the first address of the viceroy, the man created by GOD without human agency.

This place, the garden, was so important that GOD saw to it that the animals came there to see the man and to be given their names by him. It seems the man was to live in the most holy place in The Creation. Suppose for a moment that the man had eaten the fruit of the tree of life and not the other. Would it not seem feasible to assert, by extension, that the entire earth, and everything in it, would have been proofed thereby from corruption?[7]

The Final Surety

The failure of the viceroy to preserve the purity of the representation of his Father, the Creator, led to his expulsion from his intended home in the most holy place and the beginning of corruption in the earth. From that time, the ground of the earth was cursed in such a way that provision would take work effort, as had not been true before that event. The earth would now demand the attention of the man and it would begin its long, slow decline. That is why it is in "anxious longing" for the "revealing of the sons of God."

At the same time, the failure of the viceroy resulted in his decline as well. He would no longer have fully the image and likeness of

GOD. He would have to work diligently for his provision. He would be expelled from the holiest place and no longer have access to the tree of life.[8]

To be sure, the man would now be redeemed in some sense in the sons that came forth from him. They, however, would never dwell in the holiest place. Nonetheless, they would become, with Adam, a line of keepers of the knowledge of GOD; a line of priests. I argue this line of priests is the same as the "order of Melchizedek," of which JESUS is the eternal High Priest (Heb. 5:1-10).

In time, Man's corruption in the earth led to a judgment from GOD in the form of a great flood that obliterated all human life except for the priest of his time (Noah, his three sons, and their four wives). A great cataclysm came with the flood that reshaped the surface of the earth and the relationship between land and sea. The charge to represent GOD faithfully remained through that great time of natural upheaval.

A few years later, a great upheaval of mankind took place as well. This occurred at a place called Babel. GOD did not destroy Man but dispersed Man. The mechanism of that dispersal is still felt today as new ethnicities emerge and strife between ethnicities spreads to the whole of mankind. There are wars and rumors of wars everywhere (Mt. 24:6).

Each ethnicity is characterized by a culture. Each culture must be unique in some of its elements or the political purposes of the ethnicity won't be recognizable. In this mechanism, men continually draw power to themselves rather than living in the provision of GOD. The culture of the kingdom of GOD is swept aside in such an environment–or so think power-seeking men.

A New Culture

There is a culture of the kingdom of GOD. It was kept through all this early history of mankind by particular persons who were called and equipped to do so by GOD. This has been the history of these men.

In time, the men who kept to the culture of GOD would be called upon to be a holy nation to stand in the world in obvious contradistinction to the various cultures of men.[9] Such a nation would be expected to represent GOD and not be like other nations. These are the ways of GOD.

In the end of the matter, this nation would be a spiritual nation rather than a "natural" one. Its culture would be one that is spiritual in nature. This nation will inhabit a new holy place (Rev. 3:12) that is far superior to Eden. It will eat from the tree of life. It will fulfill the original mandate.[10] The sons of GOD in this nation will be unlike men in other cultures. First, though, they will need to become sons of GOD in a world that is sometimes hostile to their emergence. But the whole creation is waiting for their coming forth just as they themselves learn to groan for the finishing of the redemptive work which will result in their full adoption as sons of GOD.

---

[1] This quotation is from Isaiah 46:10. It is a favorite saying of Sam Soleyn, who has deeply impressed it on me. It is true and from both directions. The beginning was made to fit the needs of the end.

[2] He was not perfect in the same sense that GOD is perfect. Rather, no fault could (yet) be found in him and he had been created in the image and likeness of GOD with the purpose that he should rule in GOD's stead in the earth. He was perfectly suited to the task set before him. At the time of his creation, there was nothing in him to cause him to fail. He was both qualified and innocent. GOD assured that he could succeed, but with the condition that he should choose to be a son of GOD in all things.

[3] The records would survive the various eras to come down to the time of their promulgation as scripture. That those records were written is almost certain. Wiseman has demonstrated conclusively they were recorded by different persons at different times. See P. J. Wiseman, *Ancient Records and the Structure of Genesis*, (Nashville: Thomas Nelson Publishers, 1985).

[4] This is important because man is such a mess. His fallen state does not argue for accurate preservation of the knowledge of GOD. In the absence of GOD's attention it would soon be the case that GOD would be recreated so many times that He would be virtually unknown. We await a corporate spiritual man who maintains an accurate and authentic position before GOD.

[5] Revelation 22 speaks of this tree of life and its placement in the New Jerusalem. Genesis 3:22 implies the power of this tree. Even GOD respected what it could do.

[6] In that sense, the mercy seat upon the ark of the covenant simultaneously existed as a seat of GOD, specifically the throne of GOD as seen in Revelation 4:2.

[7] But instead, The Creation has been subjected to futility and it groans for the restoration that is to come with the revealing of the sons of GOD.

[8] The tree was not again seen by a human being. It will be seen when it returns with the New Jerusalem as prophesied in Revelation 22:2.

[9] *Birth of The Holy Nation, Volume 1*, and C. Gaulden, *Birth of The Holy Nation, Volume 2*, (Chambersburg, PA: eGen, 2016) offer an extensive examination of these concepts.

[10] Revelation 2:26 speaks of sons of GOD ruling the earth just as Adam was originally charged to do. The redemptive work of GOD assures their success.

INDEX

TO CONTACT THE AUTHOR

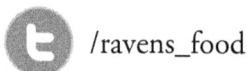

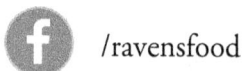

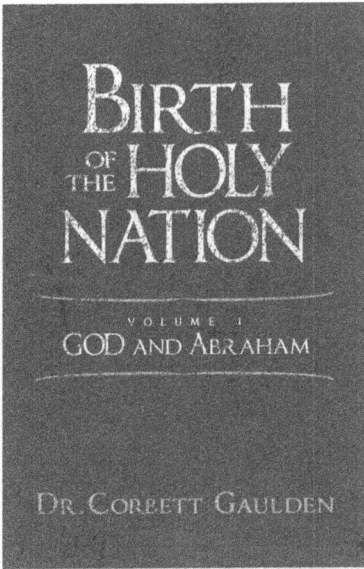

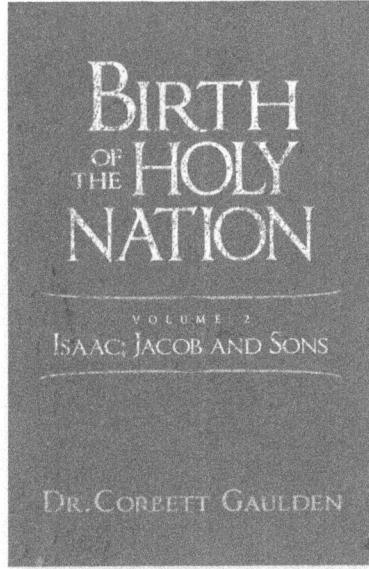

Even the most casual of students of the Bible know about the patriarchs, whose stories comprise the majority of the Book of Genesis in the Old Testament. And many others who are not as familiar with either the Bible or the term "patriarch" have at least heard the names Abraham, Isaac, and Jacob.

These three flawed and ordinary men occupy honored places of significance in God's redemptive plan for humanity through the ages. Yet many Christians have little more than a superficial acquaintance with these figures, and therefore little understanding of their timeless importance.

In *Birth of The Holy Nation*, (in two volumes), Dr. Corbett Gaulden provides an in-depth analysis and examination of the biblical patriarchs and reveals their critical role in fulfilling God's promise to Abraham, the first patriarch, to make of him a great nation that would be a blessing to the whole world. While this is a story that has been told before, Dr. Gaulden approaches it from a unique perspective, by revealing how God chose to carry out His master plan of human redemption across many generations through the basic yet complex (and some might say fragile) "fabric" of the human father-son relationship, which (ideally) reflects the heavenly FATHER-SON relationship between God the Father and Jesus.

Available wherever books are sold

THE BEGINNING FROM THE END

WHY GENESIS?

DR. CORBETT GAULDEN

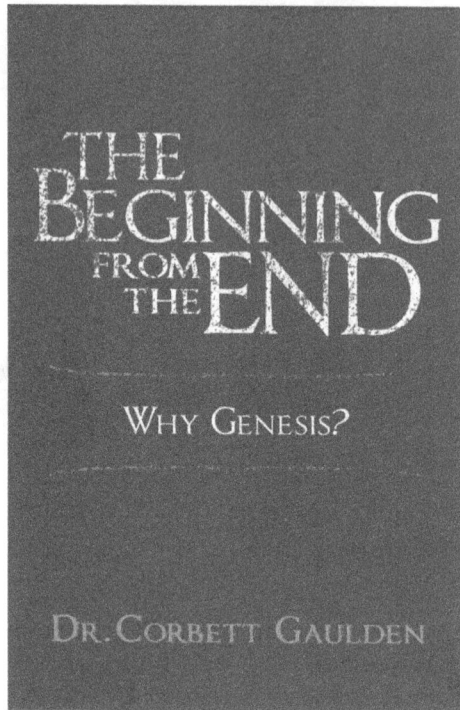

In the midst of today's heated debate over the origins of the earth and its life, including humanity, there is always a need for calm, carefully reasoned examination of the pertinent facts. *The Beginning from the End* admirably serves this need. Dr. Corbett Gaulden provides a coherent, text-centered analysis of the first eleven chapters of Genesis that is neither philosophical nor primarily theological in orientation, but rather allows the text to speak for itself, seeking to explicate its meaning in its plainest sense. As a starting point, he pre-assumes, as Genesis does, that GOD IS THE SOURCE AND DIRECT CAUSE OF EVERYTHING THAT EXISTS.

He builds his argument around four basic declarations:

- God exists and is the Creator of The Creation

- God pre-existed The Creation

- God exists in The Eternal, which pre-existed and is independent of The Creation and is the uncreated source of the created substance of The Creation

- God was purposeful in His acts of creation

The crux of Dr. Gaulden's argument is that love was God's first and most basic motivation for The Creation, and that mankind was His end purpose—a family of "sons" who would enter freely into an eternal love relationship with Him.

Available wherever books are sold

Traditional marriage is under attack today as never before. Amid the shrill rhetoric and partisan bickering, the need is great for a measured voice to remind us of the fundamental truths. Corbett Gaulden is such a voice.

Deliberately eschewing politics and focusing on Scriptural teachings alone, he takes us back to the beginning, to the origin of marriage in God's design. He then unpacks the distinctive properties that characterize biblical marriage: particularity, oneness, permanency, fidelity, a nd p urity. R egarding roles and relationships, marriage is not about power, but proper function. It is not a political arrangement or a social construct, but a spiritual institution. Biblical marriage is about covenant, not competition. It is about primacy, covering, and order in a partnership of mutual consideration. Ultimately, human marriage is a picture in the natural of the relationship between Christ and His Church in the spiritual.

Scripturally grounded and practical, *Marriage: Finding God's Design* reminds us of what much of modern culture has forgotten, that marriage is God's idea, and it functions properly only when it operates according to His standards.

Available wherever books are sold

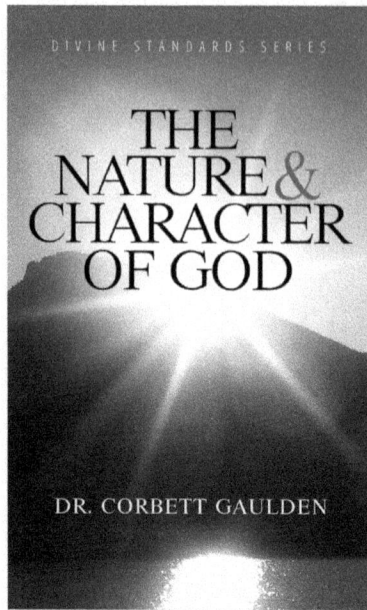

THE NATURE & CHARACTER OF GOD

DIVINE STANDARDS SERIES

DR. CORBETT GAULDEN

"Before anything else was, GOD *is*. When all else ceases to have being, GOD will *be*."

This is the simple yet profound premise behind Dr. Corbett Gaulden's brief treatise on GOD the Father. In four short but insightful chapters, he examines certain aspects of the nature and character of GOD as revealed in the specific attributes of His existence, His authority, and His love. Fundamentally, GOD is first in all things. He is first in existence, and by and through Him all else exists. As Father, GOD is first in precedence (though not in essence) over JESUS His Son.

As to authority, GOD's authority is original authority; all other authority, in the spiritual or natural realms, is derived or delegated authority received from GOD.

As to love, GOD is love; all love originates in and emanates from GOD. His love is universal, yet individual; particular and reciprocal, as modeled in the love demonstrated between GOD the Father and JESUS the Son.

Existence, authority, and love originate in GOD the Father and, as He sees fit, emanate from Him to whomever He chooses.

Available wherever books are sold

www.ingramcontent.com/pod-product-compliance
Lightning Source LLC
Chambersburg PA
CBHW060317050426
42449CB00011B/2523